8.95

The New
FEMINIST TAROT

A powerful insight into the practical application of the
tarot for personal growth, spiritual development and
planetary protection.

D1529373

The New
FEMINIST
TAROT

Jean Freer

THE AQUARIAN PRESS
Wellingborough, Northamptonshire

First published 1982 as *Toward a Reclaimed Tarot* (Lamia
Publications, London)
This revised, expanded and reset edition first published
1987

British Library Cataloguing in Publication Data

*Freer, Jean
The new feminist tarot. — Rev., expanded
and reset ed.
1. Tarot
I. Title II. Freer, Jean. Toward a
reclaimed tarot
133.3'2424 BF1879.T2*

ISBN 0-85030-563-2

*The Aquarian Press is part of the Thorsons Publishing
Group*

Printed and bound in Great Britain

HEAR
THE WORDS OF
THE UNIVERSAL MOTHER:
KEEP PURE YOUR HIGHEST
IDEAL; STRIVE EVER TOWARD IT.
LET NAUGHT STOP YOU NOR TURN
YOU ASIDE. FOR MINE IS THE CUP OF
THE WINE OF LIFE AND THE CAULDRON
OF CERRIDWEN. I AM THE MOTHER OF ALL
LIVING. MY LOVE IS POURED OUT UPON THE
EARTH. I AM THE BEAUTY OF THE GREEN EARTH,
THE WHITE MOON AMONG THE STARS,
THE MYSTERY OF THE WATERS AND THE
DESIRE IN THE HEART OF WOMON.
BEFORE MY FACE LET YOUR INNERMOST
BEING BE ENFOLDED IN THE RAPTURES
OF THE INFINITE. KNOW THE MYSTERY
THAT IF THAT WHICH YOU SEEK YOU
FIND NOT WITHIN YOU WILL NEVER
FIND IT WITHOUT. FOR BEHOLD I
HAVE BEEN WITH YOU FROM
THE BEGINNING AND I
AWAIT YOU NOW.
BLESSED
BE.

CONTENTS
Page

List of Illustrations

ACKNOWLEDGEMENTS

I have many ♀ to thank for this book:

Gillian Love-Taylor who gave me my first Tarot pack and shared her understanding of the cards with me and who years later urged me to send a copy of my Tarot book to Fay Franklin at Thorsons.

Gilly Salvat, Jackie Bat-Isha, Lyn Stevens & Janet Pearce who encouraged me to explore the Tarot.

Lindsay River and the ♀ of Cefn Foellat who stimulated my intuition.

Frances Howard-Gordon and her husband, Jaimie, who let me give Tarot readings in the back of their shop in Glastonbury for two years.

Sanghadevi and most of the other order members of the FWBO for their tolerance when I read cards for ♀ on retreat.

Philippa Berry who provided me with the opportunity to read cards in Fez.

Viv Brindson and her family who gave me true acceptance and somewhere to live.

Su Cuthbert who let me use her wonderful house in Bath where I wrote the section on the Major Arcana.

Sheila O'Reilly for her friendship and generosity.

Lee, now with the Peace Convoy, who helped me find the words to describe the way I shuffle the cards.

Sheila Wilson who commented on the journey of life and gave me emotional support in hard times.

The many many ♀ who shared their perceptions of Tarot with me, especially those who attended my Tarot classes.

All of those for whom I have done readings.

Maria Schuman, Fiona Gardner and the rest of the Bath Feminist Writers Group who helped me choose a title and cover design for the first edition and commented on parts of the manuscript.

Chris Wilson, also of the Writers Group, who prepared the screen for the cover of the first edition.

Sharon, Maggie and the other ♀ of the now defunct Bath Printshop where the original cover was printed.

Sandra Whilding at whose house I duplicated and collated the first edition.

All the ♀ I paid to help me type, proof, lay-up, print, bind and distribute.

The wide diversity of ♀ who responded so positively to the first edition.

Angie Cuthbert whose sensitivity to the cards at the age of four strengthened my faith.

Wendy Hitch whose magical beingness and unfailing love sustained me.

Jana Runnalls whose practical nature helped to earth this book in its present form.

Fay Franklin, my editor at Thorsons, who has been immensely encouraging and supportive.

The ♀ of the Grove of the Compassionate Mountain who make the work so real.

FOREWORD

HOW DO YOU SPELL WYMN?

Since the early 1970s women have been re-shaping society to include a place for ourselves within it. Much of this change has been through language. The word 'woman', meaning wife of man and referring to that portion of the species supposedly formed from Adam's rib, has especially been a focus for attention. Preferring 'woman' absolutely to 'lady', many differently spelt variations have arisen. It was Margaret Storey, who, over several years, evolved the form 'wymn'. The spellings I use reflect and address what I perceive to be particular states of consciousness and attitudes about our realities. For example, as I understand womben, they adopt a fertility-oriented definition of themselves and relate to the world through their wombs whereas wimmin and wimin refuse to prioritize childbearing and are strongly aware of the political oppression of wymn by sexism in patriarchy. A womon-loving womon is powerful and centred in herself and many womyn are consciously tuning in to our magical energies and the need to act as healers. Women share their lives with men and seek equality and a balancing of the feminine and the masculine. For me all these different spellings and others yet to be created are like the names of different tribes or clans. As wymn become more autonomous we begin to differentiate and to take on more distinct aspects and characteristics. The varieties of spelling mirror the richness of wymn's culture that is now emerging as we give birth to ourselves in this time of universal transformation.

JEAN FREER

CHAPTER ONE
WHY STUDY TAROT?

THE OCCULT TRADITION

A small number of feminists are also involved in reclaiming the Western occult tradition. The knowledge of the universe hidden in these sciences reveals itself to everyone who learns the relevant language. Thus the tradition is occult only because most people don't have the interest or make the time to study its symbols. Modern culture denies the meaning and power contained in the tradition and so most people today scorn occult pursuits. However the Western tradition, which differs in certain aspects from that of the East, has never completely died. And as with everything, the surviving occult lore must be reinterpreted in view of our reclaimed womyn's heritage. I have indicated a Dianic direction for this work particularly in the goddesses associated with each Tarot card and in the information given about numbers.

The Western occult tradition is strongly influenced by Egyptian and Jewish magic, overlaid with Christian symbolism and doctrine. The Egyptian tradition is concerned with the goddess and the god, and the yearly sacrifice of the latter to ensure the well-being of the community of life. The creation of Qabala, or Hebrew mysticism, was the work of Jewish priests, who called themselves rabbis or teachers, in the last centuries of the Age of Aries. These mystics realized the importance of the feminine and incorporated it in the concept of Binah. This is similar to the Eastern concept of yin, in a cosmology of duality. In neither place does the fe-male have the possibility of autonomous existence. In many other respects early qabalists reflected in their secrets the attitudes to women and the memories of pre-patriarchal societies current in their environment. Matrilineal descent is an indication of Jewish mystical awareness of women as the sacred sex, though the social customs incorporated in Jewish law countered any power women might touch through magic, and assured the containment of the fe-male in Jewish society.

The seventh, eighth and ninth centuries of the present era saw major changes in the interpretation of symbols and the practice of ritual in Western Europe. This time marked the first real period of strength of the Christian church which brought about a transformation of architecture, thus effecting a change in the basic harmonics of social life. Music, number, colour, alphabets and calendars had always had correspondences that, if understood, could reveal the meaning of life and give the querent power to influence it. The Christian glamorizing of suffering and glorification of dragon slaying continued the ideology of the oppression of women. Knowledge of the runes began to decline at this time, and the idea of healing was slowly being permeated with a belief in the necessity of sacrifice.

The Renaissance and the birth of modern science was a serious set-back for the occult. Students of the Western tradition are just now, with the arrival of the Aquarian Age, receiving adequate support for their researches to begin to recover lost knowledge from 600 years of deliberate obscuration and ignorant misunderstanding. One of the more recent attempts to revive the Western occult tradition was made by the Order of the Golden Dawn. Originally an Hermetic Order, dedicated to the arts of Hermes, Thoth or Mercury, this group was influenced by late nineteenth century German politics and the sexual obsessions of the period.

The Order worshipped Goddess and admitted women to its ranks. It was founded in 1888 and had strong Masonic, Rosicrucian and Theosophical links. The members of the Golden Dawn studied together, shared ritual and influenced the growth of other occult groups in Europe and America. Its members shared a vivid interest in the Qabala, and most subsequent occult work including that of many feminists follows this lead in spite of its patriarchal bias. At least three male members publicly issued Tarot decks, all using women artists to execute the designs. The group was damaged by personality clashes and internal power struggles and eventually abandoned Hermeticism to return to the safe confines of the Christian church, changing its name to the Holy Order of the Golden Dawn in 1903. From then on its influence waned and in 1914 it ceased to exist. In its time members included S.L.M. Mathers, Aleister Crowley, Florence Farr, W.B. Yeats, Paul Foster Case, A.E. Waite, Maud Gonne, Papus (Gerard Encausse), and W. Wynn Westcott.

Dion Fortune has done much to stimulate continued interest in occult pursuits and many feminists today study her work, or that of Aleister Crowley. The latter I find extremely suspect as Crowley was a renowned misogynist committed to sex magic. He changed the Strength card in the Tarot deck to Lust and glorified woman only in her aspect of the sacred whore. While as feminists we recognize the desire and necessity of sensual experience, I question the wisdom of adopting such a one-sided view of our potential. Crowley also advocated the use of drugs for instant access to mystical knowledge, a path I feel can be misleading and more dangerous than one based on patient practice and self-discipline. Dion Fortune, once a psychoanalyst named Violet Firth, accepts the necessity of heterosexuality and believes women's primary task is to be a refining influence on men. She has written many books which provide a good introduction to esoteric studies.

Women in the Theosophical Society, notably its founder Helena Petrovna Blavatsky, as well as Annie Besant and later Theosophists such as Vera Stanley Alder, have also written books which can assist anyone who is interested in approaching the occult. I believe an understanding of this hidden wisdom is essential for any of us who wish to be equipped to meet the challenges of the late twentieth century.

ORIGINS OF THE TAROT CARDS

Tarot cards themselves have been known in the west since 1392 when Jacquemin Gringonneur supposedly painted a set of cards for Charles VI of France. Seventeen of these cards are today in the archives of the Bibliothèque Nationale in Paris. Italian Tarot cards have a continuous hystory since 1441 (or 1415 according to Alfred Douglas) when Bonafacio Bembo painted the Visconti Sforza deck for the Duke of Milan to commemorate the Duke's marriage to Bianca Maria Visconti. It is presumed that these artists took their symbolic images from some pre-existing source, though today that source is lost. The earliest published references to the Major Arcana of the Tarot are a description written either in 1480 or 1587 in Latin, a late fifteenth century description in Count Maria Boiardo's *Tette Le Opere* and an Italian reference to the game of tarocchi in 1526. The pictures of the Major Arcana as we generally know them today stabilized by 1748 in the deck referred to as the Marseilles or Classic Tarot.

There are many theories about the origins of the Tarot. One favourite theory is that the deck is of Egyptian origin, representing the primeval hieroglyphics of the Book of Thoth, having been preserved in Egypt at the time of the destruction of

Atlantis. Antoine Court de Gebelin, a Protestant Pastor Freemason and satisfied patient of the hypnotist Mesmer, introduced the Egyptian hypothesis, believing as he did that the trumps or Major Arcana cards are symbolic pictures of the structure of the world. Many other writers backed this up with stories of paintings and carvings in the pyramids and other Egyptian temples, and these stories were repeated by numerous occult writers and circulated widely. Followers of the de Gebelin theory include P.D. Ouspensky, a student of the Russian mystic Gurdjieff, who had no doubt that the Tarot 'is the most complete code of Hermetic symbolism we possess'. Dr. Gerard Encausse, a young French doctor who wrote on occultism under the name of Papus, considered Tarot to be a book of the primitive Revelation. In his book *The Tarot of the Bohemians* he states his opinion that the deck is a summary of the whole teaching of antiquity. According to this interpretation, Tarot was saved from obscurity by the Gypsies, whom Papus honours with deep respect. Unfortunately many now feel the case against the Gypsies travelling from Egypt has been proved, and the current belief is that they arrived from India, making their way westward after being driven from India in the early fifteenth century by Timur Lenk, the Islamic conqueror of much of central Asia. Therefore, while it is possible that Tarot arrived in the west with the Gypsies, it is more likely that the cards arrived here in time to be Europeanized before the Gypsies themselves began to use them.

Another very popular theory about the Tarot cards is that they are a symbolic representation of the Tree of Life, containing the secrets of the qabalah. In 1856 (or 1861 in some sources) Éliphas Levi, or Abbé Alphonse Louis Constant as he was known 'in private', wrote a book entitled *The Doctrine and Ritual of Transcendental Magic*. In this book, while accepting Tarot as unveiling the 'enigmas of the sphinx', Levi also revealed its connection to the Qabalah. He associated the twenty-two letters of the Hebrew alphabet to the twenty-two cards of the Major Arcana, a practice still used by many people. Others working in the Jewish tradition see Tarot as Torah in synthesized form. The method of Qabalist Tarot interpretation has been used not only by Levi, but also by Paul Christian, Oswald Wirth, Papus, C.C. Zain, McGregor Mathers, A.E. Waite, Aleister Crowley, Paul Foster Case, Dion Fortune and Sally Gearhart and Susan Rennie, authors of *A Feminist Tarot*.

A few writers, among them some feminist interpreters of Tarot, claim a pre-patriarchal pagan origin for the cards. These writers assert that, as the ancient wisdom was progressively suppressed with the burning of libraries and later of women, the secrets were encoded in symbols and painted on cards to keep the faith alive and enable it to be shown to others. Z. Budapest, a Hungarian feminist witch living in California, says a story told to her by her mother places the creation of the cards about 4,000 years ago at an international conference near Alexandria. Another version of this story advanced in the 1920's by Paul Foster Case places the conference at Fez in 1200 C.E. As Fez is the spiritual centre of Islam, I believe this story merely serves to emphasize the relevance of Tarot mysteries to the Muslim world. From my personal experience of reading Tarot for Moroccans in Fez I can verify that although the current ('original') pictographs are European, their spiritual significance is also accessible to those steeped in Arab culture.

I feel all of the various ideas about the origins of the Tarot cards show that Tarot can be taken to mean whatever you wish it to, and that the deck can represent whatever set of beliefs you adhere to. The failure of people to properly divine the true message of the cards is due to the loss of psychic powers and spiritual wisdom in the world generally during the last few thousand years. As a system of secret symbols, obscured to protect their users from persecution, the process of obscuration has been double-edged. For with time even those entrusted with the preservation and perpetuation of the mysteries forgot their true meaning, and only a re-awakening of our deeper awareness can unlock its secrets today. I believe Tarot does reflect an oral tradition of womyn-loving times which is being reclaimed and brought up to date by womyn returning to goddess in the Aquarian Age. The Tarot deck is a memory aid which, if properly understood, will lead to spiritual regeneration.

DECKS AVAILABLE TODAY

There are numerous Tarot packs available on the market today. Most of them are versions of either the Classic Tarot or the deck painted by Pamela Coleman Smith under the direction of A.E. Waite for the Golden Dawn and issued in 1911, now published by Rider. The Classic Tarot set out the standard images for the Major Arcana and represents the Minor Arcana with the appropriate number of elemental symbols, without additional pictures. This is the usual occult procedure, which leaves the perceptions of the reader unhampered by the visions of another interpreter. Decks which follow this pattern include the Marseilles Tarot, the Spanish Tarot, the Italian Madonni Tarot, the I.J.J. Swiss Tarot, and the Egyptian Tarot. Oswald Wirth's Golden Dawn Tarot also has unelaborated

Minor Arcana cards. Richard Gardner, a prominent figure today in pagan circles, follows this path which is also used in the modern Tarot of the Witches. The New Tarot adds geometric figures to the pip cards. The Grand Eteilla Tarot, referred to as the Egyptian Gyspies Tarot, has unadorned Minor Arcana cards and in addition has the advantage of being designed before the advent of the Golden Dawn. Although Bill Butler says the designs in this pack have 'little relation to the standard deck' I find all the usual Major Arcana cards represented, with a refreshing absence of patriarchal bias in a number of them.

1. Major Arcana Card IV — The Elder

Pamela Coleman Smith was an artist with strong psychic vision. The deck she designed, considered on scant evidence to incorporate the 'original' Tarot images, is faithful to the basic fifteenth century and later Marseilles packs in its Major Arcana. It also has illustrations for the Minor Arcana which are intuitively received images. These illustrations have influenced many people's interpretation of the Minor Arcana, and many decks have repeated the use of her images with minor variations. Some of these are the Royal Fez Moroccan Tarot, the Mexican Tarot, the Aquarian Tarot and the Morgan Greer Tarot. The latter two decks were actually designed by men, a rare phenomenon until recent times. The B.O.T.A. (Builders of the Adytum) Tarot drawn by Jessie Burns Parke for Paul Foster Case, who founded an American affiliate of the Golden Dawn, leaves room for you to colour the cards yourself, though it deviates but little from Smith's designs.

A deck which has gained a wide following in recent years is the Aleister Crowley pack, drawn by Frieda Harris. I have referred to Crowley elsewhere. His cards are very large and filled with many colourful and often abstract images. To the knowledgeable eye, these cards are over-full and scatter rather than focus energy by their degenerate use of symbols. Crowley's system is based on a revelation he had in Egypt, when he pronounced that 'Do as thou wilt shall be the whole of the law'. A powerful man and influential occultist, Crowley's word was able to supercede for many the ancient law which is 'Do as thou wilt and harm no one'.

A new feminist Tarot pack has been designed in America by Billie Potts, who was schooled in Crowley's system, as her card designations and some interpretations indicate. This deck also leaves room for the individual to add to the cards, and offers alternative versions for a few of them. The first attempt to visually reclaim the Tarot, the New Woman's Tarot has been an inspiration to many of us.

Another Tarot pack to emerge recently from America is the Dakini Tarot. Designed in San Francisco, these cards do not retain the usual elemental suits, though the authors offer the correspondences in their accompanying leaflet for those who wish to study them. This deck reflects many of the concerns of our society, is humourous, optimistic and very colourful. People who are drawn to Crowley's deck, but want to avoid the spell of his particular magic, often find the Dakini pack equally satisfying.

Another unusual deck is the Sybilline Tarot, a set of fifty-two cards each representing a particular aspect of the personality. These cards are based on the oracles of the Roman sybils and are a survival of the Sybilline books consulted by Roman priests in times of difficulty. They are not widely used today.

Traditionally, in Tarot decks, only the Major Arcana and court cards are illustrated, the other minor cards just showing pips of the appropriate element. Such decks encourage a clearer psychic perception because one's intuition is not influenced or 'guided' by someone else's impression, conceived and set down in a particular time and space. Even the images of the court cards can have a restrictive effect on your understanding of a querent's personality. And repeated use of specific images empowers them in both the personal and collective unconscious, gradually confining psychic vision to pre-determined channels. I have, therefore, felt inclined to select examples from a range of decks to help free our deep mind of conditioned response patterns as regards tarot, for I believe we need, at this dawning of the Age of Aquarius, to reconsider even our archetypes. I would very much like to develop a Tarot deck to accompany The New Feminist Tarot and would appreciate hearing from any womon with drawing skills who would like to create a deck with me.

DEVELOPING OUR POWERS

Why study Tarot? Though you may have felt drawn to this book, chances are you're still not sure what it is that draws you to the cards, nor what the energy is that is reflected in them, enabling Tarot to help us see life more clearly. I want, in this book on Tarot, to explain the relevance of the cards for women today without sounding mystical. I believe in the power of women, wimmin, womyn, wimin, womben, and in the creative ability of our faith in one another. Solar patriarchy is crumbling and the poverty of masculist philosophy is being revealed. A time of transformation is upon us. The cards can help us find our way amidst the confusion and fear that abounds in our culture.

I believe Tarot is useful to ♀ today primarily because we are learning to reclaim and develop our psychic powers and the cards can assist us in this. Energy manifests itself through form. Form existing through time creates pattern. Interweaving patterns generate rhythm. Rhythms are the harmony of the cosmos. All beingness vibrates, thus expressing its energy. Energy vibrations of each moment of existence influence the future. We can view future possibilities through the forms created by the energy — as in the fall of the cards in a Tarot spread. These pre-material or etheric patterns can be changed before they are set. The awareness of possible or likely occurrences, if current trends are allowed to continue, is the foreknowledge that enables us to plan adequately for our needs. As Hawaiian Kahuna magic teaches, the more a channel for energy is travelled, the stronger it becomes. Our intention for the future definitely effects its unfoldment. Hence the importance of only giving our energies to that which we wish to accompany us into the self-created future. It is with this insight that we integrate people and nature, earth and heaven, space and time, receptivity and creativity. This vision is an entirely new quality of life.

The realm of the intuitive has never been completely stolen from us, nor can our access to it be totally closed, but we have lost our true relationship with our oracular sense as a result of years of being silenced and caged by patriarchy. Wymn's rituals, music and dance are ways in which we touch our power and achieve sufficient attunement to interpret the signs and discern the meaning of the omens. Another way to attune, to harmonize yourself with your psychic power, let your intuition flow, get in touch with your inner voice, is through meditation. I prefer sitting meditations as, for me, stillness is an attribute I seek to attain. Others prefer to achieve meditative states through jogging daily, practising Tai Chi or playing a flute or drum. Whatever is your way, tuning in to yourself will enhance your alchemical strength. New ideas are communicated by the channels we open within ourselves and time spent doing these things is valuable in itself. Experiencing another dimension in these ways has other repercussions on our lives. It helps us to realize the value of disciplining ourselves and developing our talents — what psychologists and the new age healers call personal growth. Doing this gives us more effectiveness in our lives, something we as women are particularly keen to have. Developing new strengths also helps provide us with a sense of purpose, something we need to combat boredom and depression. The cards also help us to recognize areas in our lives on which we need to concentrate.

If we stop here, we meet what I continually refer to as the dangers of egotism, a weakness plaguing the women's liberation movement as much as the rest of society. For personal power doesn't necessarily improve the quality of life — until we change our social environment we can only hope to get better at slinging shit, or manipulating chemical filth. We understand the more obscured message of the cards if we stretch to reach faith — an abiding trust in the universe to sustain life and a personal commitment to support all that is life-giving in the world. Here politics meets spirituality and women's values emerge in a political context. We can no longer deny that we are engaged in articulating an ethical morality and our success or otherwise will determine the future. We ain't got it easy but we got it, and I believe we must be as aware, responsible and courageous as we possibly can. For me, maintaining unceasing consciousness of goddess is an ever-nourishing source of strength.

Many women ask why we should bother to study Tarot. Some feel we have no need to study because we know all we need to know intuitively. Others feel Tarot is unscientific and illogical and therefore a waste of time. Still other women believe Tarot and other readings are superstitious fancies, and their fear of psychic power keeps them away. Some women, aware of the spiritual journey of life and following a path themselves, consider the use of Tarot cards ignoble.

In the world today, there is immense spiritual hunger. The planet itself is experiencing a crisis which will determine whether Gaea can survive and, with her, her children. Feminism is now recognizing the spiritual aspect of our liberation struggles, and the return of goddess to the world and in our daily lives is an integral part of achieving freedom. Patriarchy has allowed the triple goddess to remain in certain small corners, among pagans and magicians, guarded by the wizard or warlock, and glorifying the woman as lover and mother, always accessible and giving. The fourfold goddess, encompassing child and destroyer as well as maiden and crone, has all but disappeared. Though our intuition can tell us much, our conditioning is so thorough that our 'natural instincts' have been distorted and need to be placed in the clearer atmosphere of esoteric knowledge. Too much water can be vague and confusing; an integration with air, in the first instance, will bring refinement of awareness. Those who deny the power of psychic energy and cling to science confuse reason and logic. Reason is one of our innate mental faculties; logic is the particular rigid and dogmatic structure into which patriarchy has forced it. The linear sequential progression so favoured by masculists is being discarded by those seeking unity. Thus air, too, needs to be mellowed/tempered with the other elements.

Psychic power is very strong, and women are wise to approach it with respect. Denied for so long, our force repressed and resisted, we can at first be tempted easily by the exhilaration of exercising our magic. And so long awash with water, denied our fire and air, our earth expression limited by the social convention of nuclear family domesticity, we can easily become fearful and superstitious. A spiritual commitment can help to develop the faith necessary to overcome fear and the discipline of practice necessary to avoid superstition. The centering of our psychic ability in a spiritual commitment to the fourfold goddess is the surest way to avoid patriarchal exploitation of our reclaimed energies. For myself, and for a growing number of other womyn, we live with Goddess through the Dianic Craft. Those who consider the pagan life ignoble, and who despise the healing and prophetic power of witches, deny the ordinary needs of most people. Not everyone can meditate for several hours a day, yet spiritual awareness can still be available to them. It is rare that a reading reveals something the querent has not already known. The validation of her perception of what is happening in her life, and the highlighting of certain issues, is what helps her to continue with renewed sense of purpose. What may look like fayreground fortune-telling from an ivory tower may be the opportunity of ordinary women to amplify their inner voice above the noise and jumble of their busy existence.

Tarot is a tool to help us see the pattern and rhythm of our individual and collective spiritual evolution. Studying its symbols will heighten your awareness of form, number, astrology, the elements, the seasons, pattern, space-time reality. This consciousness will make us stronger materially as well as mentally and psychically, and can help to focus our will. Our strength shall make us free. We are beginning to learn true limits and to ever move towards the transformation necessary to liberate ♀♀♀ and to save life on earth.

CHAPTER TWO
HOW TO DO A READING

CHOOSING A SPREAD

The spread you choose for any particular reading is obviously very important. For only by choosing the appropriate spread can you locate the information the querent is seeking and provide the support she needs to resolve her difficulties, find meaning in her existence, realize her potential and experience joy. The first thing to determine is how many spreads the querent would like during the sitting. If you are charging money or requesting barter for your work, you will need to complete these negotiations before you begin the psychic work.

If the querent is troubled by a specific difficulty, it may be best to ask a question. Explore the querent's confusion with her, trying to get her to be as specific as possible about what she wants to know. Either/or questions are not well adapted for Tarot readings; what will happen if/when questions are best for the cards. If the question is simple, involving only one or two basic factors — a yes/no question like 'Will I win the raffle?', 'Should I go in to college on Thursday?' — the Seven Card Key is best. If the matter is more complex — 'Is my relationship going to survive its current difficulty?', 'What will happen if I change my job?' — the Solar Cross is the best spread to use. Help the querent get to the heart of the matter by repeatedly asking 'What do you mean by "X"?' about the different words she uses in formulating her question. She must ask about her own life and activities, as it is her cards you will be reading. When she has arrived at her central concern and formulated her question, remind her to focus on it while you prepare the cards.

In reading questions in the cards you are entering the realm of fortune-telling and had best consult the law, particularly the Vagrancy and Fraudulent Mediums Acts. You must also be aware that it is very difficult to precisely foretell events to come, even with clairvoyance. This is because of our limited understanding of reality, which is conditioned. Another danger with reading questions is that it provides an opportunity to pry into the querent's privacy which would give the reader a great deal of power. Most of us are still unable to handle such power wisely and so it is best to let the querent formulate the question herself, silently in her own mind, if she can.

If the querent has no particular problem on her mind she will want to use one of the spreads that characterizes her, or that looks at her life over a period of time. The spreads usually used for characterization are the Eighteen Card Gypsy Method, the Lunar Cross and the Horseshoe Spread. The Horseshoe Spread is a typical 'Fortune-Telling' spread, giving a relatively superficial look at the querent, her situation and her future. The Eighteen Card Gypsy Method is for more serious seekers who want to develop a meaningful understanding of their energies and their potential for development. The Lunar Cross provides an insight into the querent's mystic life and her potential revelatory experience. This spread and the Gypsy Method both provide a glimpse of the querent's previous lives. If you are doing the first reading of a full consultation, the Gypsy Method is the best to begin with. It is also a good spread to use if you are giving the querent her first-ever Tarot reading.

Time is always difficult to be precise about in psychic work, yet people who have their cards read are always keen to see the future. There are four spreads available to look ahead with, the most basic being the Zodiac Spread which gives an overview of the coming year. This is a good spread to use at certain Festivals. The most helpful spread, in my opinion, is the Stone Circle which looks at the present phase in detail. Depending on the forces acting in the querent's life, this covers anything from a fortnight to six months, usually indicating developments over the next three months in the querent's personal and social relationships. If the querent has her cards read regularly this is the most useful spread to use. For an occasional reading, either of the Pyramid Spreads, looking at the next few years, is available.

Your choice of spread will be determined by the querent's needs and your sense of what would be best in each situation. Decide which spread you are going to use before you finish cooking the deck, to give the cards time to align themselves in the order necessary to present their message.

PREPARING THE CARDS

When you first take your cards from their protective cloth wrapping they will be cold, unresponsive to the energies of the moment. If you do a reading with a cold deck the cards may fail to reflect the subtleties of the querent's situation, or may even speak of other matters entirely. So always begin by warming up your deck, shuffling and cutting until you feel it is 'awake' and tuned in to you and the surrounding environment. This is also an opportunity for you to focus on the cards and to prepare yourself as well. The times you shuffle and cut will depend on your assessment of the energies brought by the querent and is entirely an intuitive response.

The method of shuffling is a matter of personal choice. I shuffle with two hands simultaneously. I divide the cards and hold one half of the deck in each hand so that my hands cover the length of the cards. I place my thumb at one end and three fingers at the other end with my index finger bent and placed in the middle of the top cards. Using my thumbs I lift the front of the cards, pressing down with the index finger. Releasing the cards with the thumbs a few at a time alternately I let the cards drop, mixing the facing ends with one swift movement. Then, holding the mixed ends still with my thumbs, I raise my index finger, lift the pack and bend the cards by pushing down and slightly in with my fingers so the cards form an arc. Letting the bottom cards drop I release my fingers enough to let the other cards fall, bringing the cards back into one pile. In shuffling this way only the backs of the cards are visible. Many people associate this kind of shuffling with gambling and some feel it is not appropriate to handle Tarot cards in this way. I personally feel it helps to contain the energy within the deck, prevents it scattering or being vampirized. Shuffling in the more usual way, taking some cards in one hand and dropping them on their sides into the rest of the deck held loosely in the other brings all the pictures in turn out into the unknown open space between you and the querent. If you shuffle like this be sure to surround the cards with a protective circle of light. Many people have strong psychic power and enjoy establishing a secret competition with the Tarot reader, trying to impose their energy on the cards and distort your reading. Protect both yourself and your tools with the relevant visualizations.

For similar reasons I do all the shuffling myself, inviting the querent only to cut the deck, and when necessary to select a significator. This prevents your deck getting muddy with lots of different energies, and makes it a clearer channel of communication for you as the reader. This discipline does generate more responsibility for you, because it means that in order to get the querent's energy into the deck you must clear your mind and open a channel between the querent and the cards via your third eye and your hands. Doing this while you are cooking the deck again helps to prepare you for the reading to come through the inevitable attunement that occurs.

It is best not to make conversation during this process, though if the querent is nervous and you want to give her the chance to speak, ask if she has had her cards read before and if so whether she found it accurate and/or helpful. The purpose of Tarot reading is to help people live their lives more effectively, not to establish yourself as the best-yet card diviner, so guard against introducing a competitive atmosphere with this question. You will need to look at the cards as you are shuffling them and this will help to direct attention away from social masks and onto more meaningful patterns of presentation.

When the deck is 'cooked' and you feel ready to begin the reading, ask the querent for her favourite number. If she doesn't have one, or if you are preparing the cards for the second or third spread in a single consultation, have the querent select a number for the reading. For example, the querent's favourite number may have been used first for the Eighteen Card Gypsy Method, the number she feels is most active in her life at the moment might be used next for the Stone Circle, and a random number for the Seven Card Key used to summarize a full consultation. When the querent has selected a number, continue to focus your attention on her and shuffle the cards as many times as her chosen number indicates. This completes the process of attunement. Now immediately place the cards in front of the querent to cut.

Cutting is another matter of intuition, teaching and personal style. Some people say cards should always be cut with the left hand. Others say the hand used depends on the nature of the reading, the information you are seeking. The number of times the cards are cut also depends on one's occult education, and what you are trying to accomplish in a reading. It is possible to leave the choice entirely to the querent, placing the cards in front of her and saying merely: 'Cut, please'. Most people will cut at once, leaving the deck in two piles. Some will reunite the deck after cutting, and may even pass it back to you. Those with more arcane knowledge may have developed a personal ritual for cutting the cards and be pleased to have the opportunity to proceed unhampered. A few people will ask what to do. In general, unless I have indicated differently in discussing a spread, I have the querent cut ONCE. This creates the cosmic significator which is now at the bottom of the pack and ready to be brought out and read by you at the appropriate time. (This does not apply in the case of the Seven Card Key where the cosmic significator is the card remaining *on top* of the deck after shuffling, before cutting.) The careful preparation of the deck makes this definitive method the clearest and strongest expression of comsic influence available. However you decide the deck is to be cut, make the choice of how many cuts you are going to ask for early on in your preparation of the cards for each spread, and be clear in your intention on this matter while you are shuffling. If you are confused this will be reflected in the cards. When intending to read a cosmic significator in my experience one cut is best. In spreads where this card is not needed (The Eighteen Card Gypsy Method, the Lunar and Solar Crosses, and the Twenty-One Card Pyramid), a variation on the method of cutting may be creatively used.

When the cards have been cooked, shuffled to the querent's number and cut, lay the spread with the cards face down on the cloth. If you are going to use an individual significator in the reading, now is the time to fan the deck and invite the querent to select one. Immediately she has taken a card from the deck, suggest she turn it over and have a look at it. This card is the significator and represents the querent. Read this card as soon as it has been chosen. If the cosmic significator is to be used, take it from the bottom of the deck now and read it. Then proceed with the rest of the reading. Be sure, in turning up the cards, that you do not invert them.

After a consultation, it is necessary to clear the deck before beginning to prepare it for readings for a new querent. When clearing a deck, first shuffle five times and cut once. Then shuffle and cut several more times to numbers that intuitively present themselves to you. When the cards feel ready, shuffle six times, the number of harmonious movement and cut twice, then immediately shuffle and cut once more. If the deck is still not clear, shuffle and cut a bit more and then shuffle eight times, the number of approach, cut twice and again immediately shuffle and cut once more before putting the deck away or asking the new querent to choose her number.

GENERAL GUIDELINES FOR INTERPRETATION

For the sake of clarity I have used the term 'the querent' to refer to the person whose cards are being read. 'You' generally refers to the card reader, and 'one' or 'one-self' means both 'you' and the 'querent'. All of these terms can be read as

'your-self' which may help bring the meanings closer to you.
    I read cards at outdoor festivals and in public bazaars and
must be prepared to read for anyone who sits down. I use
several decks, and keep each of them wrapped in silk to
prevent psychic vibrations getting into or out of the decks.
Indian silk squares are available very cheaply. I occasionally
use a deck of thirteen card suits (i.e. without Kings) to read for
lesbian feminists but even for these wimmin it is often best to
use a full deck. We exist in the context of our hystorical
circumstances and reflect our environment, which means that
we today are living in patriarchy and are heavily conditioned
into accepting its misogyny (womon-hating), competitiveness,
and hierarchical and bureaucratic ideals. An individual who
has decided to call herself a lesbian feminist and may be
struggling to overcome her conditioning must nonetheless
contend with patriarchal energies. Thus, a complete deck is
often best to use. For similar reasons I never use only the Major
Arcana or the cards of just one suit to do a reading.
    If you read cards for men it is necessary to have all
fourteen cards in the minor suits. Queen energy appearing in a
man's spread shows that he is becoming more sensitive to
others. The ten of wands, a difficult card for women is a positive
card of growth in a man's reading, showing he is learning to
control his energy, not letting it wantonly escape into the
environment. Knights and Kings remind men of their
conditioning in patriarchy and the need for a strong ethical
character to resist being molded into an excessively yang, rigid
dogmatic and insensitive being. Pages and most pip cards
show humility and receptiveness, which indicate the possibility
of meaningful learning and growth. A high proportion of court
cards in a spread shows an excessive use of personality,
obscuring truth. Weaknesses of egotism and hierarchical
tendencies must be warned of with Major Arcana cards such as
The Alchemist and the Keeper of the Mysteries, dangers to
which men are particularly prone. Similarly Strength may
merely be brute force in an unevolved subject. The Initiate,
The Moon and the three of cups show a man getting in touch
with his feelings and developing his intuition, possibly
honouring goddess in his life. Willing to learn from women,
only if he is not secretly ripping us off will such an individual
receive the gifts of goddess in his life. The interpretation of
Tarot presented in this book will only appeal to those who truly
support the liberation of women and the return of Goddess to
the world. These people may well be aware of C.G. Jung's
work on archetypes and be interested in Richard Gardner's
work with the Tarot. Though both of these men seem overly

involved with fixed polarities, they nonetheless encourage others of their gender to develop their receptive intuitive aspects.

Always sit directly in front of the cards, cross-legged on the floor or if in a chair with your feet flat. Have the querent sit facing you with the cards directly in front of her. In this way the cards and the cloth they are on occupy the space between you. This enables a cone of power to be raised which will help psychic forces to reach the intuitive awareness of both reader and querent.

When doing a reading, interpreting the individual cards is only the first step. After reading each card, patterns of relationship between them must be sought. This is mostly an intuitive insight, though certain guidelines can be given. Be aware of repeating numbers. Any number which appears three times is making a statement in its own right. If all five cards of a particular number appear (four pip cards and the relevant Major Arcana card) the message is pointed indeed, and cannot be escaped. Look, too, for relationships between the numbers. If the spread consists mainly of pip cards and these are the lower numbers one to four, the querent is just beginning to develop the energies indicated, putting down roots and establishing habits and patterns for herself. Such a time is delicate, requiring caution and gentle nurturing if the opportunities being presented are not to be lost. A preponderance of eights and nines indicates concerted effort and realized creativity in a context of goddess orientation and womon-spirit. Sevens and tens together create a more patriarchal energy while fives and sevens show chaotic movement. A pattern of sixes and eights indicates easy pro-gress in the most fruitful channels of development available to the querent.

Always count the elements in a spread, as a sign of the degree of integration of the querent's energies. If one element is noticeably predominant the querent will benefit by focusing on that energy. If an element is missing entirely the querent is likely to be experiencing dis-harmony, dis-ease. However, this is not the case when asking a question. Absence of an element in one of the question spreads indicates that energy is not involved in answering the question. An element may be in a minority in a spread, but represented by strong flexible cards which show that particular element does not need direct attention from the querent for the time covered by the reading, and that those energies will reliably support the querent while she is learning the lessons of another element or combination.

Water and fire are known as the two creative elements. Be

aware of the relation created between these two elements in each reading. Occasionally numbers repeat only twice in a spread, and you may find three or four pairs of numbers in a given reading. Though numerically this is not particularly significant, look to see if the pairs repeat a relationship of elements, say always being pairs of cups and wands — the creative elements, or cups and pentacles — traditionally female elements. Note the placing of the elements in a spread and again be aware of the integration or otherwise of the querent's energies.

Also consider the court cards present in the spread. If they are proportionately plentiful the querent relies on her personality to achieve her ends. Kings and Knights indicate aggression and a need for dominance. Kings and Pages show an either/or personality which swings between extremes. Inverted Knights indicate self-abuse or, rarely, particularly intensive focus on inner development. Queens indicate a fully realized personality. Inverted Queens may reveal bureaucratic tendencies.

Attention must be paid to the number of Major Arcana cards, their element, their placing in a spread and whether they are inverted. The four dragons — the Keeper of the Mysteries, Death, The Thunderbolt or Lightning Flash, and the Earth Dragon — are particularly to be looked for. They represent a special intensity of experience, and are directly linked to the soul evolution, developing karma, or spiritual awareness of the querent, helping her to discern the meaning of her own life. Sometimes the Major Arcana cards will all appear in the area of inner work, leaving the querent's outer life appearing quite bland. In other spreads they will create a thread running from the querent's past to her future, or from her unconscious roots to her conscious preoccupations. A high proportion of Major Arcana cards in a spread indicates an intensity of energy, marking the period covered by the reading as a very important one for the querent. This is especially true at the present time as we are moving into the new age of Aquarius. Many people have incarnated now to help humunkind through the difficult transition we are now experiencing. Most of these modern avatars have been slowly preparing themselves, some have been stalling; all of us were hoping for a bit longer to get ready. However THE TIME IS NOW and all who can serve are being called upon to do so. Each of us may still refuse if we choose to, though the opportunity to make this choice is unlikely to come again, even though it may already have presented itself to us several times before. A querent at this crossroads in her life will have a high proportion of Major Arcana cards appearing in any readings she has done.

The affiliations or correspondences of the Major Arcana cards will assist you in interpreting them. You may find that your work with Tarot leads you into a study of mythology and astrology, and later perhaps to numerology and alchemy. The philosophy contained in the cards is deep and meaningful and can help us to achieve the calm and power necessary to live happily on this earth. The study of the cards, including meditations on their images, is a path of self-development that will help us to live in harmony with the timeless universal forces of life.

Astrological correspondences are particularly to be considered. Cards linked to the cardinal signs (The Moon, Justice, The Elder, The Alchemist) show the ability to initiate, and may be somewhat flamboyant or dramatic. Cards of the fixed signs (Judgement, The Star, The Matriarch, The Sun) have a holding power or stubbornness which convey an ability to survive. These cards may also indicate a willingness to destroy in order to achieve a resolution. The mutable cards (The Initiate, Love, The Wise Womon, The Chariot) indicate the ability to work away at a matter until its heart is reached, though a scattering of energy is also possible. The personal planets are indicated by Strength, The Wheel, Hanging, and Temperance, while the outer or social planets are the four dragons.

Look at the numbers you assign to the Major Arcana cards and correlate these to the numbers of the Minor Arcana cards in the spread. Remember that each Major Arcana card in the second portion of the lemniscate has a minimum of two numerical values. Take some time with a reading to allow these patterns of relationship to emerge.

If all the Major Arcana cards in a spread are of the same element, the querent is working specifically with that energy during the time indicated by the spread. Usually dispersed throughout the elements, such a concentration of Major Arcana cards is likely to mean the querent has been blocking that energy in the past, inhibiting her creative power, and that she will now unavoidably experience the force of the elemental energy in her life. Such an experience will help her come to terms with that aspect of herself. If the querent already knows the energy, the focus of Major Arcana cards in the element means she is going to evolve a new and more meaningful understanding of that power in her life which will hugely enhance her effectiveness.

Particular combinations of cards also provide information about what awaits the querent. The five and ten of the same suit indicate that the querent has overstructured her energies there and will inevitably have to handle a shake-up in that area of her life. The five of cups and the five of swords together show that a relationship in the querent's life has ended but she is not yet ready to accept the reality. The five of swords in the querent's outer life accompanied by the seven of cups in her inner life may indicate someone in cloud-cuckoo land, or a manipulator who lies to others in order to make her fantasy life seem more real. Be aware of combinations appearing in the readings you do, and let them assist you in divining the message of the cards.

2. Minor Arcana — Two of Cups

Querents will often ask if you can see anything about their health or their love life, or whether they will move home or change job. It is unlikely that any one card will hold the answer to these questions; the patterns the cards make together can reveal to your psychic self the possiblities latent in the situation. If there are no cards reflecting relationships showing in a spread there will be no major changes in the querent's emotional life during the time being looked at. If there are no water cards in a Solar Cross asking about a relationship, the partnership in question is not actually concerned with emotional energies at the present time. If someone wants to know if a change of home is indicated, several signs could be sought. The most basic is the Knight of Wands, traditionally the change of home card. However, even if this rider does appear, it is wise to look for supporting evidence, for the Knight of Wands also means taking your creative energy out into the world, possibly through preaching/ teaching, and having an influence on the environment. So a querent with this card may be changing the focus of her creative effort, rather than actually moving house. Other change of home cards could be the five of pentacles (material upheaval) or the ace of pentacles (new material beginnings). The seven of pentacles together with the Knight could be a very strong indication, showing that the querent is going to create the living space she desires. Warn of excessive ego if this combination appears. Ace of wands and six of pentacles could mean moving home, or a new attempt at sharing of material resources, which could renew the querent's optimism about collective living. Many other indications are also possible; the reader must be guided by her intuition in seeking them out for interpretation. Develop your own codes to look for an answer to these needs.

The question of inverted cards is a subject of much discussion as is the meaning of retrograde planets, both phenomena being symbolically similar. Traditionally, that is, since Renaissance times, inverted or upside-down cards have been interpreted as having the opposite meaning to their ordinary, upright sense. To my mind, this understanding of reversals is a perfect example of polarized thinking, creating extremes that are forever alienated from one another. It is possible to ignore reversals completely, and still derive significant and meaningful information and guidance from the cards. If you do disregard reversals for the time being you may find that in two or three years you will have developed a better insight into why they occur in different places and at different times in readings you do for yourself and others. (Be sure in turning over the cards to reveal their faces that you merely 'open the door'; do not upend them, thus inadvertently reversing them.)

My understanding of inverted cards is predominantly that they indicate inner work the querent is doing on herself. When these cards appear in areas of the querent's outer life they show that the querent is seen by others to be working on herself and developing her inner life. She is likely, too, to be consciously endeavouring to integrate the demands of her inner and outer lives. In rare cases inversions indicate that the querent has only a mundane consciousness and is not aware of being involved in a process of spiritual development, thus rendering such readings meaningless to her. These cases are infrequent, and your decision as to whether inversions refer to the process of inner alchemy or not rests entirely on your INTUITIVE perception. I cannot emphasize too strongly that when doing Tarot readings it is vital to READ THE CARDS; DO NOT INDULGE IN PSYCHOLOGY. Things are usually not what they appear, especially in the lives of people who consult oracles, and it is an offence to the integrity of your clients to read their cards according to your understanding of their social mask. Remember, it is a seeker sitting with you and you are a channel for communication between her and the unseen world in which her spirit lives.

Inverted cards also warn the querent to guard against the dangers associated with the particular card and as a reader it is best to mention these potential weaknesses, challenges or difficulties when interpreting inversions. You may also point to strengths in other cards that will help the querent to avoid the pitfalls of which she is wise to be aware. In a similar vein, inversions show blocked energy and the querent may expect frustration and possible delay in the areas of her life indicated by reversed cards. Nonetheless these times also provide the opportunity to go over something again, allowing the querent to develop a more precise understanding and heightened awareness of the matter. This can impart a timeless or eternal quality to the experience.

Particularly with Major Arcana cards, reversals indicate a lessening of intensity along the lines of blocked energy, though possibly without such immediate conscious awareness of frustration. The strength of experience indicated by the Major Arcana can be excessive for many querents at various times in their lives and inverted cards shield the querent from the full force of the energy indicated.

However you choose to interpret reversals, or the meaning of the cards in general, you will find that if you are consistent in your interpretation the cards will yield up their meaning to you.

The purpose of consulting the Tarot is to help us become more aware of the energy patterns in our lives. Even if we see difficulties ahead, our foreknowledge can help us be better prepared to meet the challenges as they arrive. There is no need to be fearful of the messages brought by the cards. Every reading should leave the querent optimistic about her life, and feeling better able to live it to her full potential.

CHAPTER THREE
THE MINOR ARCANA

NUMEROLOGY

Numbers are very significant and every tarot reader, regardless of her formal schooling, has a knowledgeable theory of numbers. The variety of these theories is good evidence of the different versions of truth and reality which are used by people today. Compare, for example, the meaning given to the number five: to some it means upheaval, change and disruption while to others it means marriage and reunion, to others difficulty and defeat. The ivy leaf sacred to Kali has five leaves, we prototypically have five fingers and five toes. $5+5+5+5 = 20; 4(5) = 20; 20 = 2 \times 10; 2+0 = 2$. Already a variety of form has arisen from the single idea 'five'. Such an idea, one which has taken on or developed the power to generate form, can be called an IDEATE. I have discussed the political power of Ideates in an earlier book. (*Further Thoughts on Feminism or What Is To Be Done?*).

To help you in the development of your own understanding of numbers, I have given a basic meaning for each number, and key words for each card in the Minor Arcana, by suit. Thus, four represents unity, harmony, stability and wholeness which in the suit of swords can be understood as an alchemical rebus. The rebus symbolizes the creation of new thought forms through the combining of different points of view. Such a stage is very necessary in the alchemical process, as practising Hermeticists and other students of the occult will know from personal experience. The weakness of the four of swords is mental laziness. Thus in each suit is the unitary theme of four given its particular elemental essence. In this way does one discern the differences between gnomes, fairies, devas and sirens.

The court cards — page, knight, king and queen — represent yet another point of view. Though they are to be considered as 11, 12, 13 and 14 they have additional meaning as personality cards. The personality is a much misunderstood aspect of our being currently given a great deal of attention by so-called scientists of the emotions.

Psychology, which has carved its territory out of the traditional field of spiritual occultism, tells us most of what is generally believed today about the personality. Rooted in materialism, with the over-emphasis on emotions which characterizes the Piscean Age, this new science has distorted our perception of ourselves. The will, the ego, our inner beings and our outer face are all distinctly different, though they merge into a confused mass in most of us. The personality is our outer face, shaped by our other selves and conditioned as well by our physical bodies. With discipline we can determine for ourselves how we use our energies and, consequently, what our shape will be. Without discipline we will remain undifferentiated and confused, perfect subjects for psychological analysis.

There is also the question of whether each suit was originally 12 or 13 cards with one or two added later. If this were so, which cards are the late arrivals? Only the Queen and the Page, or Princess, have always been there, child and mother. Either the knight or the king, or possibly both, could have interposed themselves. It is likely that the knight entered first and then became the king, as Zeus was first introduced as Hera's brother and later became her consort and oppressor. This tradition is repeated in the legend of Marian, Moses' sister who was kept alive in the alchemical maria, or heated bath, and reappeared in Catholicism as Mary, by then meaning bitter. Isis is returning today as herself and the emergence of the Dianic tradition testifies to Her enduring strength. If you remove the kings to have a 13 card suited deck, be sure to consider the possibility of the kingly attributes of rigidity, dogmatism and self-control in any Queens that may appear in a spread.

Numerology of the Major Arcana was originally unspecified. With the entrenchment of a linear sequential thought process, the cards have acquired a set of such numbers. I have attributed these numbers to the cards in accordance with my own understanding of their qualities. It is possible my perception of this will change over time. I believe my choice of numbers for the cards can be best understood when the Major Arcana is laid out as a lemniscate, the sign for infinity which is an eight laying on its side. The first egg or tear drop is the creation of the individual. The second is creation of relationship with the eternal/universal. The Wheel of Fortune is subsequently crossed by Judgement, and the World and the Fool stand either side of the point of intersection. This is a power point.

Each card in the Major Arcana represents a quality of experience. An individual does not progress rigidly through the lemniscate in the unidimensional time line of her life. We do live in a variety of time spheres simultaneously, a topic beyond the scope of this book, and in some of them the sequentially numbered lemniscate does represent a symbolic pattern of growth. This pattern shows a lifetime's development and is repeated within the overall cycle in a variety of expanded and contracted ways. Equally, each individual card holds a variety of experience which gives it depth and breadth, the spiralling essence of life. It is in these concentrated experiences that the essential quality of the number assigned to the card becomes most meaningful.

All two-digit numbers carry two numerical values, that of their face number and the value of the number which is the sum of the digits. Thus sixteen is itself, and seven $(1+6 = 7)$. It is also twice eight, the number of apprenticeship and conscious application repeated for emphasis in the context of a structure or practical form. For those involved with the Dianic tradition the value of this number is four times four, the whole and stable universe resonating with the harmony of realized goddess consciousness as well as thirteen plus three, reclaiming our ancient foresisters and returning the power of womyn to the world by the dynamic activity of the Triple Goddess of sisterhood. The number assigned to the Earth Dragon, this card is of particular relevance today.

Each of the numbers can be examined in this way, with or without reference to the Tarot. The vast network of relationship that exists in the world of numbers soon becomes apparent. The number itself, the sum of its digits and the various numerical combinations — through both addition and multiplication — which can create it must all be considered. As this is not a numerology book I have restricted myself to a brief description of the basic number, and a list of key words for the cards themselves.

THE NUMBERS

ONE   new beginnings, birth or rebirth, and renewal of energy. One is the seed, and contains all possibilities for the future, though it has only a tenuous existence — not yet rooted.
Symbol: a point

TWO   generating power, putting down roots. Twos
               represent a temporary balance, and the danger of
               polarizing.
               Symbol: a line

THREE   dynamism and connection. The plant is
               flowering, putting its energies out into the world.
               The active aspect of life. Over-emphasized by
               Western patriarchy.
               Symbol: a triangle

FOUR   harmony, unity, stability, completion. Fulfilled
               creation, the fruits of effort. The contemplative
               aspect of life.
               Symbol: a circle

FIVE   dramatic change. A shake-up that will create
               space for growth. A crisis in everyday life due to
               the changing nature of existence.
               Symbol: a star

SIX   harmonious movement and growth of
               awareness. Moving away from recent difficulties,
               though perhaps with a tendency to look back.
               This number represents personal evolution.
               Symbol: an arc

SEVEN   the key, the number of magic. Beware of egotism
               and illusion. Seven taps unseen power sources,
               touching your infinite potential. Abused by
               patriarchy in the Western occult tradition.
               Symbol: a spiral

EIGHT   approach, apprenticeship, getting closer to your
               chosen goal through application. Putting your
               power in a moral context.
               Symbol: a lemniscate

NINE   pure energy flowing in unblocked channels.
               Quintessential experience, intense creativity. A
               special goddess number.
               Symbol: an ellipse

TEN   excessive structure, impeding the flow of energy.
               Stable, but absorbing energy that could otherwise
               be used creatively. A primary patriarchal form.
               Symbol: a square

THE COURT CARDS:
Aspects of the Personality

PAGE, PRINCESS, VALET, KNAVE:
receptivity, humility and openness. Vulnerable and impressionable. May try to lead too soon.

KNIGHT, AMAZON:
assertive, arrogant, ready to fight if necessary. (Choosing a favourable time in which to fight is a sign of strength.) May be too worldly, insensitive and out of harmony.

KING, PRINCE:
rigid, dogmatic, fixed and authoritarian. Controlling. Can be self-control.

QUEEN, COMPANION:
sensitive and stable, providing security for herself and those around her. Creative. Can be indulgent.

THE ELEMENTS

WATER represents the psychic sphere of existence. It is the element of our emotions, our desires, our intuition and our memory. Creativity and peace express themselves in water. Cups is the suit of water.

The element water corresponds to our astral bodies and appears as sirens or undines. The element of mysticism, water is the medium of birth and rebirth. Assigned to the West and spring, wells, rivers, springs and lakes convey its power. Water is the special province of Cerridwen.

AIR represents the mental sphere of life. It is the element of our intellect, our rational understanding, our esoteric perception and our mental abilities in the occult sciences. Mathematics and astrology communicate through this element. Air is also the element of love. Swords is the suit of air.

The element air corresponds to our mental bodies and appears as sylphs or devas. The element of occultism, air is the medium of visualization and revelation. Assigned to the East and autumn, incense and wind convey its power. Air is the special province of Ishtar.

EARTH represents the material, manifested sphere of reality. It is the element of our physical bodies, our tangible environment, our practical work and our finances. Pentacles are also a sign of magical protection. Imagination and beauty express themselves in earth. Pentacles is the suit of earth.

The element earth corresponds to our etheric bodies and appears as gnomes. The element of geomancy, earth is the medium of sense experience and manifested magic such as conjuring entities. Assigned to the North and summer, salt and barley flour convey its power. Earth is the special province of Demeter.

FIRE represents our will, the energy we use to get things done. Free will depends on liberating ourselves from the demands of the ego, allowing our personality to be an expression of our inner spirit. Our fire is also the source of our compassion. Wands is the suit of fire.

The element fire corresponds to our spiritual being and appears as elves or fairies. The element of alchemy, fire is the medium of purification by reduction and of regeneration through revitalized intention. Assigned to the South and winter, oil and flame convey its power. Fire is the special province of Hecate or Helle.

THE NUMBERS IN THE ELEMENTS: KEY WORDS

WATER

one	—	intuition/creativity
two	—	love
three	—	sisterhood
four	—	meditation/boredom
five	—	loss/depression
six	—	learning through dreams/music
seven	—	mystical experience/fantasy
eight	—	turning inward

nine — inspiration/contentment

ten — families

page — young love/poetry
the inner voice

knight — carrying the cup of life/
the seducer

king — guilt/emotional self-control

queen — creative imagination

THE NUMBERS IN THE ELEMENTS:
KEY WORDS

AIR

one — initiation/cutting through

two — waiting/indecision

three — encountering new ideas/
mind denying feelings

four — wider understanding/
mental laziness

five — confusion/white lies

six — spiritual evolution/moving
away from difficulties

seven — piercing the veil/trickery

eight — astral travel/mental knot

nine — occult awareness/
clear vision

ten — mental housecleaning
needed

page — astrology/gossip

knight — fighting

king — law

queen — justice

THE NUMBERS IN THE ELEMENTS:
KEY WORDS

EARTH

one — protection/self-healing

two — power/faith

three — work

four — resting/hoarding

five — upheaval/disruption

six — sharing/co-operation

seven — creativity/control

eight — practical experience/discipline

nine — quietude/comfort

ten — responsibility/authority

page — pagan practice

knight — work in the community

king — wealth and authority

queen — at home with nature

THE NUMBERS IN THE ELEMENTS:
KEY WORDS

FIRE

one — optimism/new project

two — integration

three — gathering energy/
day dreaming

four — prosperity/celebration

five — clash of wills

six — self-awareness/
egotistical laziness

seven — will power

eight — repeated effort

nine — determination/obstinance

ten — burden/self-oppression

page — psychic receptivity/
good news

knight — change of home/
creative endeavour

king — social prejudice and bigotry

queen — charisma and charm

THE SUIT OF CUPS (WATER):

ACE OF CUPS

The ace of cups shows new emotional beginnings. If the querent has been going through a difficult time, this card shows a fresh start in the emotional field, and a renewal of her optimism concerning affairs of the heart. This card also shows the beginnings of psychic power, the emergence of the querent's intuition as a source of knowledge. The recognition of the importance of a moral context for her interpretations, spiritual values to live by, is also indicated here. As this card is the first in the water series, the powers represented here are not yet developed, and must be nurtured if they are to grow. There is the possibility of vagueness as a weakness. The querent now has a new opportunity to get in touch with her feelings and to awaken her creative imagination. Pleasure awaits her.

TWO OF CUPS

The two of cups shows love entering the querent's life through her cosmic awareness and/or an earthly love affair. Sympathy with emotional and intuitive forces will aid her growth. The effect of love's alchemy may be to unite her emotions with her spiritual intention, a bonding which comes through understanding. The two luminaries — the moon and sun — mingle their different energies, shedding light on the wider mysteries of life. The querent may have glimmerings of the mystical experiences which could await her.

There is a danger of over-emphasizing romantic love, an indulgence of emotions conditioned by patriarchal assumptions. Also beware of possessiveness.

THREE OF CUPS

The three of cups is the sisterhood card. It represents emotional connection with other women, and the Triple Goddess, the

3. Minor Arcana — Three of Cups

three graces. There will be no loneliness for a querent with this card. She can expect happiness and celebrations in a spirit of love and friendship. This card may show the querent becoming involved with feminism. The flowering of a relationship with a womon-friend is indicated. Developing psychic communication between the people in a small group is also possible.

Dangers with this card include abuse by patriarchy, such as accepting a subservient or servicing role. The querent might also feel emotionally unstable, which can result from all the dynamic emotional activity indicated by this card. In this case look for some earth in the spread, and recommend that the querent ground herself with it. Beware of watery excess.

FOUR OF CUPS

The four of cups represents listening to the inner voice. The unity, harmony, completion and stability — the sense of wholeness the querent has achieved with her water energies — will give her a sense of emotional security and peace. Her inner voice will be able to provide all the guidance she needs, if she will make the space to hear it. This can be done through a practice of meditation, and by visiting sacred wells and springs and other centres of water power. These pilgrimages can inspire spiritual visions, though the querent must guard against dreaminess. Trance work is possible with this card.

If the querent does not feed her spirit when faced with this card she is likely to experience boredom, and may be prone to drunkenness as a form of escapism. The hungering spirit which is denied creates a wretchedness from which there is no escape. It is far better to acknowledge our spiritual needs and to begin to meet them. We can then hope to experience universal love, and the bliss of perfect peace.

FIVE OF CUPS

The five of cups represents emotional loss. This may mean a time of sadness, even depression, but remember that only by letting go can the space be created to change. This card shows separation from what was loved and is gone; advise the querent to allow herself to accept this experience now for if she blocks it, it will come again.

The upheaval indicated will also affect the querent's intuitive powers, making way for a new approach to psychic work. This is a time of moving through pain and confusion, thus allowing anguish to fall away in order to touch the creative powers that lie deeper within. Disappointment is inevitable in life; do not despair.

SIX OF CUPS
The six of cups indicates harmonious movement of the querent's water energies. This means increasing intuitive powers as well as emotional growth. Happiness in the querent's present circumstances is achieved partly through reflection on her past experiences. She feels her emotional life is improving. The querent should be sure to get enough sleep and allow her dreams to help her move comfortably through her changes. A querent with this card may have musical ability. This is a card of movement, progress, ease and harmony.

The danger with this card is excessive nostalgia, focusing on past happiness to the exclusion of the current reality. Though we can learn more about our emotions by reconsidering our past experiences, we must live in the present. Do not dwell on past relationships or on intuitive powers lost through lack of discipline. Learn to live without romanticism. Be rested and stay with it.

SEVEN OF CUPS
The seven of cups represents a scattering of emotional energy and indulgence in fantasy. Seven is the magic key and, when used with discipline, the querent is able to create the reality she desires. A mystical experience for the querent may be indicated. When used as a source of stimulation and excitement, the seven of cups shows emotional distractedness and delusion rather than strong intuitive powers and spiritual inspiration. Drug use, which distorts consciousness, may also be indicated here. It is important to learn the differences between imaging, creative visualization and fantasy.

EIGHT OF CUPS
The eight of cups indicates that the querent is approaching deep self-knowing. Turning inward to see oneself reflected in the deep waters within, this card reminds us of the need for psychic protection and the importance of closing our chakras each day. This can be done through visualization before getting out of bed each morning. The individual here has the opportunity to experience true illumination of the path, and to feel the creative impulses she has been nurturing begin to realize their potential. This card indicates that the querent may be approaching her spiritual goal. A journey across water may also be indicated.

When negatively aspected, this card can indicate following a false path; wrongly interpreting the psychic information one is receiving; being misled by the shadows; not going below the surface. Increasing intuitive powers can be destructive if not guided by spiritual insight and commitment.

NINE OF CUPS

The nine of cups indicates pure clear intuitive awareness and strong direct emotional energy. The querent will be feeling very creative and experiencing the powers of vibrant spirituality in her life. She may have access now to memories of past lives. Good luck is indicated. This is a card of contentment.

The danger is spiritual drunkenness or egocentric introspection. The power achieved by the querent with this card will not be lasting if she uses it only for personal gain. Also guard against excessive emotionalism or sentimentality. The contentment brought by the fulfillment of the nine of cups may undermine the querent's commitment.

TEN OF CUPS

The ten of cups indicates that the querent has a lot of people to keep happy. This situation gives her a sense of emotional stability but absorbs most of her creative energy which she could more fruitfully be using elsewhere. Her anger at this oppression is likely to lead to her making some changes in order to free some of her emotional and intuitive power for her own use.

This card is said to represent happy families and may be interpreted as showing lesbian communities. Servicing others' emotional needs in an atmosphere of resentment inhibits the development of psychic perception.

PAGE OF CUPS

The Page of Cups represents the inner voice which can be heard through the reading and writing of poetry. This voice can guide the querent in her life, and she will benefit from gaining access to it. In this way, too, the querent will begin to develop her psychic powers of mediumship. The emotional sensitivity of the querent with this card will make her receptive to the flow of energy in the atmosphere around her. She may also be in touch with her subconscious and feel the faith which has sustained her through many lives. Mystical experiences may be enhanced by meditation.

The Page of Cups also represents young love — the affection of a young person or animal, the tender love of a new relationship, or the unpretentious affection of a close friend.

Emotionally vulnerable, the Page of Cups may lack the maturity of experience which can teach us to protect ourselves. A querent with this card may have romantic tendencies and be confused by illusions which are merely reflections of her own desires.

KNIGHT OF CUPS

The Knight of Cups carries the cup of the wine of life out into the world, bringing the message of psychic wholeness, love and peace. This querent is also one who brings pleasure to others, but she may be emotionally closed and so untouched by these experiences herself. Such pleasure, though not a true sharing, can nonetheless increase the happiness in the world and have a healing influence, and the querent's desire to please is genuine even if her motives are unclear. She may be offering illusions in place of truth.

This card also represents the seducer, someone who swamps others with her emotional power, confusing them with romanticism and setting them adrift in the sea of her own reality. It is possible to seduce others in the guise of offering spiritual enlightenment, a well-tried gambit very popular now with the dawning of the New Age and the increase in the number and intensity of true and false seekers. A querent with this card must examine her intention and be aware of the principles she serves. The ego may tempt her and her desires may threaten to overwhelm her judgment. The querent may be false to others about her emotions or out of touch with her real feelings.

KING OF CUPS

The King of Cups represents emotional control. Emotional self-control is a helpful practice in self-development and is difficult to achieve without losing touch with our feelings. Permission to feel what we're feeling has only recently been given to society by the growth movement and many people, encouraged by psychology, are now awash with their emotions. Such an over-emphasis of water is the last resurgence before the passing away of the Piscean Age, during which time watery excess appeared most often as pity and guilt. The danger with this card is using guilt to gain emotional control of yourself or others. Guilt is as useless as pity in life, both serving only to block the flow of energy. Real emotional control maintains an elasticity which encourages emotional responsiveness without excess or indulgence. Emotional dishonesty is possible with this card.

This card, when positively aspected, also shows a querent who is no longer lost in the swamps of spiritual exoticism. Even when indicating rigidity and dogmatism, a querent with this card may need the inflexibility of that kind of emotional or psychic energy to cope successfully with the pressures placed on her by her current situation.

QUEEN OF CUPS

The Queen of Cups represents someone able to provide emotional security for herself and those around her. A querent in harmony with her yin energies, someone with this card may find others coming to them for advice about emotional matters. Sensitive to the vibrations in the atmosphere, the Queen of Cups is caring of the feelings of others, responsive to their needs and benevolent in her rulership. She receives the love of those around her. A sense of tranquility surrounds someone represented by this card.

This is a card of creativity, indicating artistic imagination as well as developed psychic power. At her best, the querent is able to experience a range of phenomena and emotions without losing the sense of her own identity. She experiences much pleasure and happiness in life. The querent here is mistress of herself and receives the inspiration of goddess. The cup of the wine of life is freely offered to those with the courage and discipline to partake of it wisely, and the cauldron of Cerridwen will reveal the mysteries to those with the intuition to perceive their meaning.

When inverted or poorly aspected this card can represent someone who is over-indulgent of her emotions or imagination, unable to create because of the constantly changing tides which shift them about. Such a person might tend to moodiness, imaging emotional relationships others do not perceive. Romanticism is likely to be a weakness, and the querent may have a tendency to self pity. A tendency to dominate others with the force and unpredictability of her moods could also be indicated.

THE SUIT OF SWORDS (AIR):

ACE OF SWORDS

The ace of swords indicates a victory, a cutting through of old barriers to a new beginning in air. An initiation could be indicated. The querent may be entering on a new line of study. She will feel her mental powers to be vigorous, perhaps a refreshing change after a recent period of difficulty. This card may also show a new way of perceiving reality, the beginning of a new mental understanding and new lines of thought. It may also indicate the beginning of occult study and a comprehension of esoteric knowledge. The ace of swords represents the seed of new ideas. If you nurture them they will grow.

The danger with this card is an excess of intellectualism disrupting the harmony of the whole. While reasoning is a valuable process, the use of logic, a patriarchal form, is contrary to life forces. Air energy must be integrated with the other elements if one is to truly develop clear vision. The querent's new vision may bring a sense of isolation. Look out for an illness that may be coming if the necessary precautions are not taken.

TWO OF SWORDS

The two of swords indicates a mental conflict contained by the effort of balancing opposing views or ideas within oneself. The total stillness of absolute balance requires complete concentration, an absorption within one's own mind that precludes perceiving anything without, as well as anything within yourself beyond one's own mind. This perception of true balance may therefore be a form of deceit, a way of lying to oneself or to others. Conformity may be indicated. This absorption can also lead to false displays of tenderness or concern for others which are motivated by the need to avoid physical and emotional activity in order to remain engrossed in oneself.

This state of balance through blindness, withdrawal into one's mind, truce and enforced stillness is a temporary one, associated with the new moon which always betokens change and growth. It may be necessary to avoid an inner mental conflict at this time in order to put necessary energy into other areas of the querent's life. The querent may take the opportunity offered by this mental paralysis to take up a form of meditation, a practice which uses mental stillness. The indecision of the querent's position may impart caution. She may be feeling schizophrenic.

THREE OF SWORDS

The three of swords represents connection with the mental energies of others. Reading or discussion can be the source of the connection, or a meeting of minds may occur through occult work or exercises within the mental sphere. The stimulation provided by this connection will help the querent to make progress in her understanding of reality. She may also find herself changing her associations to accommodate new thoughts.

The traditional image for this card, a heart pierced by swords, is a symbol of the Virgin Mary, as illustrated by Anne Kent Rush in her book *Moon Moon*. It represents the patriarchal reality of the mind denying the emotions as science is destroying the world. Gearhart and Rennie remind us here of the patriarchal paradox of romantic love and violence. The sword has been made solely an instrument of destruction in our current culture. We must reclaim the creative power of cutting through to clear perception and accept the necessity for cold hard vision when required for our growth. Only when devoid of other elements, or in some other way over-stressed, does a sword reading indicate danger, hidden enemies, violence or illness. The mental aspect of our being must be re-integrated into our lives on a harmonious basis.

When poorly aspected, this card can represent the patriarchal tendencies I have already indicated. The three of swords may also indicate excessive mental stimulation which can generate confusion. A change in the querent's thinking may be the cause of disagreements with others, and could lead to the severing of partnerships. A querent with this card will not necessarily be mixing with other people 'in the flesh', but will be encountering their ideas through books, lectures and discussions, while astral travelling or via occult experiences.

FOUR OF SWORDS
This card indicates the combining of various points of view into a new outlook on life. A necessary step in alchemical transformation, the creation of a wider understanding symbolizes spiritual growth. This is a time of mental consolidation, when the querent is digesting what she has recently learnt. A unity and harmony of minds is indicated though, in fact, the querent may be working alone.

When poorly aspected, this card represents mental laziness and an unquestioning acceptance of the teachings offered by others. In this regard church dogma is particularly dangerous; a critical analysis of biblical teachings will generate a rebirth of thought in a new sphere.

FIVE OF SWORDS
The five of swords represents mental turmoil, a shake-up of the querent's ideas. Threats and slander may be the cause of it. Loss or death may be indicated depending on other cards in the spread, and your 'sense' of the reading.

This card also shows the peacemaker. At best this person is able to turn swords into ploughshares. In weakness, this card represents white lies, saying what is necessary to keep the peace, to keep things running smoothly regardless of the truth behind them or the hurt they might cause. The querent will feel she is acting for the best but this is true only in a superficial analysis. These falsehoods will return to her, and the upheaval indicated by this card will not be escaped. Her cowardice may lead to disgrace.

The disruption is necessary because the querent has not yet learnt how to control her own mind, and is still mislead by false notions of reality. This is an opportunity to find a fresh approach.

SIX OF SWORDS

The six of swords shows spiritual regeneration. It is one of the most powerful Minor Arcana cards. P. C. Smith represents here the journey across water which has always signified the change from one state to another since Paleolithic (Stone Age) times. The harmonious growth of mental understanding and the clearer perception of occult knowledge indicated here reveal a significant move in the querent's spiral of personal development. She may wish to communicate this new knowledge to those close to her, who share her idealism. The querent's mental evolution will help her to a new understanding of the challenges in her life.

This card may also indicate a turning away from difficult problems in life to focus on the inner journey. Only if our inner strength helps us to resolve our outer difficulties, so that we can live in peace, can we be said to truly evolve. Refusing to learn a lesson means willfully missing an opportunity to grow. Such waste upsets the eco-harmony of the cosmos.

SEVEN OF SWORDS

The seven of swords means piercing the veil of illusion to have a more direct perception of reality. All of the querent's previous experience has now brought her to the point of seeing, without distortions, the reality of her everyday life. This knowledge will increase her effectiveness. Foresight and cunning are advised when dealing with a powerful enemy. Analysis and criticism strengthen her creative powers of visualization, and her efforts are building the future.

This card can also represent trickery, which only the querent can discern. Beware especially of the tricks of the mind.

Depending on the other cards in the spread, and their positions, surgery may be indicated.

EIGHT OF SWORDS

The eight of swords in the P. C. Smith deck shows a witch's cradle, used to facilitate out-of-body travel. The querent's occult perception is increasing and she is on the verge of a breakthrough in esoteric understanding. The answers to her questions will come to her through her experiences while astral travelling. BE SURE TO GET ENOUGH SLEEP. Though the querent is moving closer to her chosen goal, her mind is in a knot. Remember that such confusion, blindness and lack of understanding often precede the emergence of a new vision. Others may criticize her, and she may be critical of herself. Nonetheless, she is on the right path as various incidents make clear. Have faith and do not give up. Remember to sleep more when this card appears.

NINE OF SWORDS

The nine of swords shows a pure creative flow of mental energy. The querent is able to concentrate without effort and has strong insight into the nature of reality. She is likely to have developed a regular habit of meditation which helps her to guide her mind and prevent it tormenting her. Her study of astrology is likely to be well advanced and she welcomes the influence of the stars in her life, her heightened awareness enabling her to use their energies to enhance her own perceptions. Her keen vision and clear understanding give her the ability to harmonize potentially conflicting points of view.

There is the possibility of exhaustion through stress and anxiety. Do not overdo things or indulge in suspicions, as this can lead to false visions and an inability to interpret signs. This card can represent crying alone in the night for those who are unable to come to terms with the power of their own minds.

TEN OF SWORDS

The ten of swords shows excessive mental baggage which must be eliminated if the querent is to grow. Fixed ideas about reality are preventing the querent seeing life as it is, and an over-crowded mind means she has no room to learn. In this way she is generating sorrow for herself, though she may blame her troubles on her circumstances. Over-structured mental attitudes are imprisoning her and she is trying to impose her ideas on others as well.

The ten of swords is the strongest loss card in the Minor Arcana. A major change in the querent's perception and outlook on life is indicated. She may experience this death of a way of thinking as a defeat but will soon find herself to be more open-minded. This mental house cleaning will result in the letting go of a point of view whose usefulness has passed.

If you are a student, this card indicates mental congestion due to the information you are being fed, but it could indicate success in your exams.

If you are involved in psychic work this card may represent your fears of an attack, which would come from behind as your aura is more flexible there. This card is a reminder to seal your aura and take other necessary precautions to protect yourself. In battling with the patriarchy beware of accepting masculist definitions of the struggle.

PAGE OF SWORDS

This personality card represents an openness to new ideas, and may indicate that the querent is embarked on a period of study, perhaps of astrology or another occult science. An individual who recognizes words as useful tools, this card indicates an ability to think clearly about complex ideas. The querent here is clear-headed and enjoys the stimulation of mental activity. This person is a vigorous thinker. Awaiting messages is indicated.

The Page of Swords can also indicate gossip, a form of spying on others which is disruptive, destroying social harmony. The querent may feel vindictive toward those in her social circle. So long denied effective influence, women are often tempted to malicious pettiness by the frustrations of limited lives. The desire for revenge can be assuaged by the Holly Flower Remedy,* but if the querent is basically selfish she will have to examine her ideals if she wishes to change. Remember that whatever you give out comes back to you increased.

A querent with this card may want others to think as she does and therefore try to lead before she is ready. It is also possible that she may be too easily influenced by others' ideas, for which the Walnut Flower Remedy is a help.

KNIGHT OF SWORDS

The Knight of Swords is prepared to fight if necessary. She is armoured and armed — guarded and defended — and has the power of her belief in her ideas to give her strength. Her faith in her own way of thinking is so strong that she is tempted to force others to think as she does, and she may have difficulty in seeing others' points of view. A querent with this card knows that ideas have the power to change the world, and she is taking her ideas out into the world to influence the directions of this change. A dynamic figure, she often succeeds in getting others to share her ideas.

The Knight of Swords may be closed to new ideas and fixed in her own view of the world. This fixity is obscured by the fierceness of her crusading, but if left too long will become the

* One of the Bach Flower Remedies — essences which relate to the personality and states of mind.

rigidity and dogmatism of the king. The querent must be sure she is not acting from ignorance backed up only by bravado. The force of this card can easily turn to violence. The querent needs to be aware of the possible use of intimidation to achieve her ends and must judge the use of such energy in the light of her ideals. This individual is impatient, needing constant stimulation. She may start things she can't finish, deaf to the wise counsel of others.

KING OF SWORDS
The King of Swords represents closed-mindedness, rigid thinking and control through threat of legal punishment. A querent with this card is inflexible in her mental attitudes and unable to consider fresh approaches to any difficulties in her life. Possibly afraid of mental collapse, this querent is judgemental and dogmatic in her pronouncements and tries to maintain a firm control of her mind. Mental self-control can of course be an asset when maintained without fear or threat and this card may show the querent regaining her mental powers.

This card may indicate having recourse to the law, and represent a querent who is authoritarian and believes in the positive social value of maintaining law and order. Such an individual will be strictly logical in her thinking and will be suspicious of anything irrational. Sado-masochism is possible with this card and cruelty a common attribute. When having to deal with the legal system this card indicates a querent who can hold her own and defend herself without wavering.

QUEEN OF SWORDS
The Queen of Swords has a clear perception of reality and the courage to speak the truth. Because of this she may often be alone and experience a sense of isolation. Not many people are able to hear the truth, and this querent will accept her loneliness rather than compromize her vision. Her judgements are very fair though she has a tendency to be stern and must remember the weakness of humun nature if she is to be merciful in her lawgiving. She may be hardest of all on herself.

A strong-minded individual, this querent is intelligent and gains strength from her knowledge and understanding. Others recognize her authority.

This card may represent a woman recently widowed. A querent with this card must guard against becoming bitter, and be aware of any tendencies to distance herself from others.

When poorly aspected this card can indicate a ruthless individual, seeking vengeance and lacking in compassion. A woman absorbed into patriarchal modes and values may be indicated, someone who has lost her sensitivity in the strictures of legalism. This querent would support militarism and use her power cruelly.

THE SUIT OF PENTACLES (EARTH):

ACE OF PENTACLES
The ace of pentacles represents new material beginnings, being at the gate of the garden. The querent may be experiencing a change in her material circumstances, possibly receiving unexpected money. She may be feeling physically renewed after an illness. A new consciousness of the earth is indicated. The querent has realized the importance of respecting the integrity of the earth mother and living in harmony with her. She has also recognized the spiritual dogma of 'transcendence of the physical' as part of the patriarchal attempt to deny womyn and keep us down. The querent is learning to care for her body, to honour herself and the earth as different aspects of all women, in this way gaining the strength to help free us all. This card also represents the magical protection received when one acknowledges the existence of unseen forces.

When poorly aspected, this card can mean the pursuit of worldly power and material influence as ends in themselves. The instability of this card can mean that the querent is misled, unable to see the wood for the trees due to her inexperience and naivity.

TWO OF PENTACLES
The two of pentacles shows the querent is generating a new source of power within herself, at her solar plexus. She feels the strength of an integration of her material life with her spiritual life, and the rewards of physical discipline. The Fool of the Minor Arcana, this individual has the potential to attain wisdom and to learn to use her power responsibly to the benefit of womonkind. This card also indicates wages earned, and weighing up the practical possibilities available to the querent.

This card can represent a foolhardy discounting of warnings. The querent may be creating difficulties for herself by refusing to take account of the material realities of her situation. Her appetite for sensual experience may be at odds with her desire for cosmic consciousness.

THREE OF PENTACLES
The three of pentacles indicates work with others to give

material expression to your beliefs. This coming together in the material realm includes the availability of the necessary resources. Money for womyn's land may be indicated.

When poorly aspected, this card represents ill-chosen work, perhaps a project that cannot be successful at this time or one that serves the interests of the patriarchy.

FOUR OF PENTACLES

The four of pentacles is a card of material stability. Unity and harmony with the material world and a sense of physical safety and completion are indicated. This card represents receiving gifts. The querent has what she needs materially, and must look after it. Our bodies are the first gift we receive in this life and this card reminds us to care for them. Be sure to get enough rest. Only by nurturing our bodies can we expect them to serve us well in magic, in physical struggles, in the long journey of life. This card says the querent needs more sleep.

The weakness of this card is inertia, the habit of remaining immobile as if stuck in one position. The querent with this card may also have a tendency to hoard, greedily holding on to that which she has. Such an attitude is likely to generate loss in her life; we create far more opportunities to receive if we are open and willing to let energies flow.

FIVE OF PENTACLES

The five of pentacles represents an upheaval in the querent's material world, and a change in the way she presents her physical self to the world. This can be a change of job or home or hairstyle, the latter being a very important aspect of our physical presentation of ourselves in the world. The material disruption presented here can give the querent a sense of being out in the cold. She should remember that this shake-up is necessary and will create the space for something new to enter the querent's life. She is now able to learn a new way of existence.

This dramatic change may result from misconduct by the querent, and can represent broken bones. Financial stress is also likely with this card. The card may indicate spiritual hunger resulting from the querent's alienation from the natural life forces.

SIX OF PENTACLES

The six of pentacles indicates co-operation in material matters and sharing of material resources. Awareness of the interconnectedness of all existence will inform the querent's relationship to her environment, making her more conscious of the needs of the planet and more willing to act on this awareness than she has been in the past. This card shows that the querent's material circumstances are now moving smoothly, assisting her growth. She will have sufficient material resources to meet her needs. The querent may receive an inheritance.

The dangers with this card are martyrdom, or matronizing others. These mental attitudes undermine real sharing. If you feel that, by giving or receiving, you are storing up merit, you are still being greedy and ambitious and will not benefit in the manner you intend.

If the querent is a gambler, this card shows a winning phase.

SEVEN OF PENTACLES

The seven of pentacles represents the ability to shape the material environment according to your will. The querent with this card has strong magical powers, and is able to produce psychic phenomena on the material plane. Does she exercise these powers for personal aggrandisement or does she put her skill to wider use? Such power can have intense political effectiveness if used collectively. This card may indicate a change in the way the querent earns her living.

The danger here is being too involved with facades and external appearances. The querent may also believe that, without her efforts, there would be no life. Though the querent can influence the shape of reality to her design, nature would continue creating life and it would progress through its cycles even if the querent did not exist. She may be experiencing anxiety about control.

EIGHT OF PENTACLES

The eight of pentacles is the card of apprenticeship, indicating the improvement of physical skills through practice. This work can include pathworkings, and strengthening of our bodies for such work through hatha yoga or other regular discipline. The querent is now refining her ability to influence her material environment and placing her power in the context of her beliefs. Her work is bringing her closer to her chosen goal. In the realm of finances this card represents prudence and economy.

The weakness of this card is avarice, excessive materialism leading to spiritual blindness. Remember that physical health and ability are not ends in themselves, but part of an integrated approach to holistic living. A feminist approach to spirituality recognizes the vital importance of the physical body and

material existence, but does not emphasize these beyond any
other. Similarly consuming or amassing goods merely
perpetuates the power of patriarchy.

NINE OF PENTACLES

The quintessential expression of harmony with the earth, the
key word for this card is 'quietude'. A querent with the nine of
pentacles feels a peace and oneness with the forces of nature.
The ability for self-reflection which distinguishes people from
animals is properly used for self-knowledge and does not make
us wiser than dolphins nor more aware than cats. Neither does
it indicate an inferiority to monkeys or other creatures. Unity in
diversity is the essence of natural life, and a querent with the
nine of pentacles has learnt to attune herself to the natural
cosmic rhythms of life, finding her integrated place in the
pattern of the universe. She has reached her own still centre
while experiencing a vibrant and enduring relationship with
the life around her. This card represents a period of rewarding
material creativity, bringing beauty and comfort into the
querent's life.

The potential weakness of this card is self-satisfaction. The
vanity which can result may also smack of elitism based on
feelings of superiority toward those who are unable to create
such a smooth set-up for themselves. But if this is your attitude
you may be certain that your material comforts will not bring
you inner peace, and you may have to lose them in order to
return to the path of wisdom.

TEN OF PENTACLES

The ten of pentacles indicates domestic or administrative
responsibility. The querent must keep together a substantial
material structure or life-style. Though providing stability, the
requirements of precedent and tradition block the creative
expression of the querent's talents. A position of wealth and/or
authority is indicated, though the querent herself may feel
over-worked or even enslaved by her situation.

PAGE OF PENTACLES

The Page of Pentacles represents pagan practices and
indicates the querent is open to developing her relationship
with the earth, seeking to heighten her receptivity to its
messages. Taking country walks and being in the open as
much as possible are important to her. Going barefoot and
being naked out of doors whenever possible will enhance her
relationship with the elements. The querent may also be
embarking on an area of study, perhaps one that involves

practical experiments or that will strengthen her connection with nature. Serious application to the practical requirements of existence characterize the querent with this card. The extent that psychic powers are involved in this work will be determined by the querent's perceptions. She must guard against a misuse of her developing powers. The querent may be delivering or receiving letters or parcels and may have recently taken up a new line of work.

As with all pages, the Page of Pentacles is vulnerable and the querent will need to look after her health, eating wholesome food and getting sufficient exercise. She is also impressionable, and may be encouraged to spend her money too freely. Protection and guidance are available to her if she remembers to ask for it.

KNIGHT OF PENTACLES

The Knight of Pentacles represents work in the community. A politician or youth and community or social worker is likely. The querent earns her living by going out to work, and may find it necessary to protect herself, putting on her 'public image' in order to do this. The world changes the querent seeks to create are practical ones, affecting material reality, and she is not afraid of hard work. She may work directly with the land.

When poorly aspected, this card can indicate someone who is a defender of convention or obsessed with profits. Things may mean more to this querent than people and she may evaluate her friends in terms of their usefulness to her. According to Gearhart and Rennie an inverted Knight of Pentacles shows someone who has no visible source of income and yet is never in want. I interpret this Knight when inverted as representing physical self-abuse.

KING OF PENTACLES

The King of Pentacles represents the material benefits of patriarchy and control over the material world. The querent represented here derives her authority from her financial wealth and may be prone to showy displays of opulence. She may have heavy financial responsibilities which require business dealings within the patriarchy. This can mean the querent must be rigid and dogmatic in practical matters in order to hold her own in the vicious world of masculist competition. Such a stance may, however, merely create resistance and make the querent's position more difficult than necessary. Careful deliberation will help her choose the best strategy.

A querent with this card is also able to command the physical forces of the universe and so can create 'super normal' events. Nonetheless, she may be a staunch materialist and deny any awareness of the non-physical world. Such a querent lacks creative imagination and arrives at her conclusions after slow consideration of all the tangible factors involved. Her actions are 'sensible' and 'realistic'. She favours control through the use of structure and may appear insensitive. When poorly aspected, this card can represent greed and overbearing pride as well as an excessive reliance on material reality.

QUEEN OF PENTACLES
The Queen of Pentacles represents someone at home with nature. This querent is able to derive support and comfort from the material world and has the ability to make the physical world yield up to her that which she needs. Materially stable, this querent does not worry about money and is able to provide security for those around her. She is generous and protective. Living in harmony with the earth she knows the art of geomancy and practises earth magic when required.

The querent recognizes the strength of ritual in generating endurance, and will often lead ceremonies at the regular festival gatherings. The Matriarch of the Minor Arcana, this querent is creative and powerful and a respected member of her community.

When afflicted, this card shows someone who has become dull through excessive materialism and whose creativity has been limited by her practical circumstances. Such a querent may rely over-much on structure to achieve her ends and be complacent and unyielding in her approach to life.

THE SUIT OF WANDS (FIRE):

ACE OF WANDS
The ace of wands represents a renewal of energies, and possibly the beginning of a new project. The querent will feel more able to take initiatives, to be assertive in her life. The renewal of strength and vitality is likely to make her more active than previously. Diplomacy may be a keynote. This is an optimistic rebirth.

The weakness here is impulsiveness, starting things she doesn't want to see through. Also, there is the possibility of the querent's enthusiasm making her insensitive to others.

TWO OF WANDS

The two of wands shows a measuring of the demands of the inner and outer life and attempting to integrate them. The querent is aware of her ego operating through her personality in the outside world, and she can also feel her spirit pressing for recognition within her. Will is the energy she has to meet these demands and, providing it is not enslaved by her appetites, there are vast possibilities for self-realization available to the querent. In choosing where to put her energies it is important that the querent does not plan beyond her abilities for this would only create unnecessary frustration and sorrow for her.

THREE OF WANDS

The three of wands represents drawing sufficient energy to yourself to realize your projects. The querent may be encouraging others to become involved in her project, establishing a business partnership or creating a collective enterprise. If she is working alone then she is generating the necessary energy within herself, sparking her own fire. Optimism is essential here, and a belief in the importance and validity of the work to be done.

The potential danger with this card is dreaming and not doing. Endless planning can fire people up and they can feed on the flames of their enthusiasm for a time. Eventually however the querent and her friends will become dull from such repeated meaningless stimulation. The querent and others will lose faith in her if she does not use her influence creatively.

FOUR OF WANDS

This is a card of harvest, the Lammas festival, reaping the fruits of one's earlier labour. In the best circumstances this card represents joy and celebration, feasting and dancing. It is a time of peace and harmony of the querent's energies, when inner turmoil is absent, projects have been completed, she has gained control of her inner energies and feels at one with the motive forces around her.

The danger here, or potential weakness, is egotism, a smugness which denies that the querent has received help from any outside forces in achieving her prosperity and fruitfulness. Such lack of humility obscures the nature of reality, for although a seed contains within itself the essentials of its own maturity, it will not grow unless it is nurtured from without as well as from within. This card shows a time when possibilities for future development are being created within the querent. It can represent agreeing to a contract.

4. Minor Arcana — Four of Wands

FIVE OF WANDS

The five of wands shows a conflict of personalities. Depending on the place it appears in a spread, an inner conflict or a clash of wills with others will be indicated. The shake-up caused by this turmoil is usually a necessary one. If within, the five of wands represents a sorting out of the querent's priorities to make the space for fuller self expression necessary for self-realization and growth. A clash with others shows the querent is standing up for her beliefs and refusing to be bullied. If in business, this card shows the ability to stand up to competition. If other cards in the spread show the querent to be stubborn and bigoted then this upheaval will be part of a well-known pattern. A court case or law suit may be indicated.

SIX OF WANDS

The six of wands indicates increased self-awareness. Harmonious growth of the querent's fire energies is enabling her to know herself better and to unblock her energy so that her growth can progress. She is an example to those around her as she faces her fears and confronts her doubt. She is optimistic about the way ahead. There is harmony in all her efforts and her talents are growing. Her psychic powers are beginning to develop as her will becomes stronger, and she is more able to consciously direct her energies.

The danger with this card is a feeling of 'I've done it all before', the attitude that her work is over, she has nothing left to do or learn and can just 'rest on her laurels'. This attitude is especially dangerous in our struggle to overcome our conditioning. All of life teaches us continually, and an openness to life's lessons is required for true spiritual development.

SEVEN OF WANDS

The seven of wands is the card of magic, showing the force of the querent's will. She is aware of her influence. The querent is able to hold others in her spell by the power of her charisma. The use of voice is a basic ingredient of her magic. Regulating the temperature of the alchemical fires is a delicate art essential to achieving successful transformation. Women who play carelessly with their psychic power, or who crave evidence of their influence and are obsessed with seeing the effects of their work without concern for the purpose of the effort, will be burned. Free will can be one of our most effective tools in the struggle for our liberation if we are able to be mistress of our own powers in service of goddess.

The querent is feeling better able to shape her own life. She has determination and may be about to have some writings published.

EIGHT OF WANDS

The eight of wands shows the querent is focusing her energies, using them in the ways most likely to take her to her chosen goal. This card shows that things are progressing swiftly in the querent's life and that she is gaining more control of herself. She is in touch with her unconscious drives. The willingness to discipline her energies through repeated effort will soon pay off. Her creative power is growing, and she is able to influence others with her powers of persuasion. She is trying not to repeat past mistakes and rejoices in the strength she derives from the growth of her spiritual awareness.

In her impatience to realize her potential, the momentum of the querent's efforts may cause her to force developments. The pressures of the ego, though more subtle than with the seven, are still a danger. Insisting on personal control of cosmic events results in extreme exposure, and loss of protection.

NINE OF WANDS

The nine of wands is a card of intense creativity. The querent's fire energies are flowing smoothly, as round an elliptical orbit, and she is able to express both courage and compassion. The querent is in charge of her own energies and she may be experienced by those who have not disciplined their energies as obstinate or stubborn. But the womyn who have likewise been refining their energies, focusing their power and learning the true nature of their strength will welcome the querent and are likely to be excited by the possibilities of united effort. The pure expression of her will, unhampered by guilt, shame or other obstacles, makes the querent with this card very powerful. Joined together with other womyn, sharing power to create a new future, these sisters are a source of immense hope for our liberation. The strength of the querent's creative power may be experienced as pure joy. As in all such times of success the querent must guard against egotism, and beware of encouraging the development of a cult of the personality around herself.

TEN OF WANDS
The ten of wands is a card of oppression, carrying a burden for others, possibly accepting the social prejudices offered as part of the querent's conditioning. The querent is unable to give full expression to her personality. This burden is self-chosen. It is possible that the querent's love of power causes her to seek influence for its own sake, rather than in service of a principle. In such a case her own personality will be her biggest burden, as she will constantly need to support her own image in order to retain her popularity.

The temporary obstacle hampering the querent is a challenge to the strength of her determination and can be seen as an encouragement to learn to be in charge of her own energies. The situation may require the querent's powers of diplomacy, especially in matters relating to management and personnel relations. This card can provide the opportunity to learn self-control and may represent celibacy, control of the querent's sexual drives. The burden represented here may be part of the querent's karmic inheritance. Where the ten appears with the five, the querent must examine her prejudices, and be ready for a shake-up of her personality. Though this will be disruptive, it is only by experiencing this conflict and the upheaval it brings that the querent can make room for new growth.

PAGE OF WANDS
The Page of Wands represents good news, and may indicate that the querent is beginning to hear voices. There is no need to

be frightened by this phenomenon; it is best to listen to the voices and try to interpret their meaning. It is necessary to learn to distinguish real messages from illusory ones, and to develop the skill to communicate them to others as a source of healing power. It is important that the querent with this card get enough sleep, in order to be sure she is clearly receiving and understanding what she is hearing. Care of our bodies, especially sufficient rest, is essential to all psychic work and the development of our powers.

The querent with this card shows originality and initiative, and is often able to encourage optimism in others. She will be receptive to suggestions for new projects and ideas about where to put her energies. The weaknesses with this card are excessive impressionability, and undirected or unchannelled energy. The querent may also have a tendency to unnecessary theatrics.

KNIGHT OF WANDS

The Knight of Wands is traditionally the change of home card. If the querent is not actually moving house, it can represent a major change of focus, a shifting of her centre of attention. This Knight means the querent is taking her creative energies out into the world, and having an impact on her environment. The querent may be artistic. Skilled at teaching, the querent is able to convert others through the example of her personality and persuasion of her debate. This querent will also be a successful preacher, communicating fiery enthusiasm to those who come near her, and working her will on her environment. The querent's personal example is her most effective tool for change; her life is her text. She is energetic and resourceful. A charismatic figure, her impact remains behind long after she has moved on.

The intensity and swiftness of this querent can spread unrest among those she visits. Her energy can generate discontent and make her undesirable company for those who wish to lead a settled or orderly life. The querent must also be aware of being used by others as a source of entertainment — "better than television". These people have no real desire to make change and the querent can waste a lot of her energy trying to fire them to action. If she wants to spend time with people like this she must learn to hold her own power, to protect herself from rip-offs. She must also guard against the desire for excitement for its own sake and always strive to make meaningful use of her influence. This querent has an appetite for movement in her life, often experiencing separation. She has strong powers of endurance.

KING OF WANDS

The King of Wands is controlled by her conditioned social prejudice, which leaves no room for the free expression of her spirit. Lacking in compassion and a stranger to humility, this person controls others through intimidation. A forceful personality, the King of Wands can hold others in her sway, often influencing them to adopt her beliefs and prejudices as their own. A person with a short temper and given to bursts of anger, this individual's creativity is thwarted by her need for power and social status. Can be convincing in argument, through clever use of words, and has a tendency to show off. A bigoted individual may be indicated.

This card can represent self-control and the querent may be able to resist the temptation of her ego to use her charismatic personality to get what she wants. This can be an important step in overcoming conditioning but must not be prolonged as rigid social attitudes may then crystallize. A querent with this card must guard against making excessive demands of others and indulging her vanity.

QUEEN OF WANDS

The Queen of Wands is a strong, charismatic character who uses her personality to channel the creative energies of her environment. Often invited to lead, she brings a dynamism to the endeavours in which she is involved which inspires those around her. She usually achieves success and is surrounded by an atmosphere of plenty and good luck. At her best this querent is honourable and conscientious and is an example of spiritual determination to achieve her highest ideal. She is compassionate and able to counsel people well because of her sensitive awareness of social situations. This querent is independent and efficient.

When afflicted this card indicates someone who uses her charm to bewitch, to hold others enthralled under her spell. This individual is an object of admiration and envy, yet experiences disquiet in her inner being because of her selfish motives. The querent may be excessively proud and overbearingly self-righteous. Beware of impatience with self or others.

CHAPTER FOUR
THE MAJOR ARCANA
THE JOURNEY OF LIFE

It is possible to regard life as a journey, the striving of our inner being for the fullest possible realization of its potential at each moment in time. Tarot illustrates the ideal pattern of life: the spiral path of spiritual evolution. It provides guideposts on the journey of life, helping us to develop ourselves and our relationship with the world in the most spiritually evolved way we can. If we perceive the meaning of these signs, we can enhance our competence in life.

Each card indicates a quality of experience, an energy pattern characterized partly by its element, number and placing in the spread. More than that, each card represents a particular expression of the Self and symbolizes an aspect of awareness emphasized at the time the card appears. Card readings help the querent to clarify her perception and to move more effectively through her time/space.

The episodes represented by the cards of the Major Arcana can and usually do recur throughout the querent's life. Both breadth and depth of experience are possible, and a variety of approaches to each card is likely. At times the querent's energy will move sequentially through a portion of the lemniscate in a recurring progression until the momentum has done its work and the querent has been transformed. Otherwhiles a specific card will appear repeatedly as the querent delves more deeply into that aspect of herself. In this latter case the querent will repeat the experience, seeing it from a variety of perspectives, until she has fathomed its meaning. The same card appearing later in her life will indicate she is ready to understand another dimension of that phenomenon.

A primary task in life is to reconcile the demands of the inner life with those of the outer life, and Tarot shows us how to combine the habits of each creatively. Learning to be fully

alive, to awaken our consciousness and be open to the
rhythmic patterns of experience, enables us to integrate the
harmony of our individual life with the universal one.
Psychological truths are also firmly embedded in the Tarot
cards, especially in the lemniscate that can be created by the
Major Arcana. Many of us believe that life is inherently
meaningful and try to comprehend its message through our
experience. Thus, we view our circumstances in life as a
pattern which, when discerned, teaches us self-knowledge and
cosmic awareness.

5. Major Arcana Card XV — Temperance

The Major Arcana also reveal the occult knowledge and
esoteric wisdom which are seen by many as a path of initiation.
As patriarchy is at odds with these energies, so too are the
images of the cards distorted with Rosicrucian and later
Christian symbolism. The pagan gnosis, or truth, contained in
the deck is all but obscured and is only slowly being reclaimed.
Those of us moving nearer to Goddess are better able to
decipher this meaning. Arcanum means a secret and the cards
contain the wisdom of the ages which has been preserved,
distilled, protected and communicated to those with sufficient
awareness to understand these symbolic attendants of humun
spiritual evolution.

THE NUMBERS

ELEVEN   beginning again with some experience, some form. Nurturing the roots. A number of strong spiritual insight.

TWELVE   dynamic fullness, established power. The completion offered here is healing and opens doors to wider or deeper experiences.

THIRTEEN   the number of spell-casting, firmly based yet capable of creating total anarchy. Each individual must make a personal relationship with thirteen and in so doing will come to know her own true morality. The year is often repersented as a thirteen-branched tree.

FOURTEEN   magical change. This number has lost some of its magical force in the process of being confined in patriarchal structures. It is openly associated with the halcyon days of midwinter and with ritual burial.

FIFTEEN   inevitable movement. The energy of fifteen is unable to remain still and so is characterized by continuous change and completeness. The full moon occurs on the fifteenth day of each lunation.

SIXTEEN   intelligent application. Consciousness of work. Sixteen is the true road to effective transformation and is a number of increase. Relating your spiritual hunger to your physical world you are able to combine elements to create and evolve.

SEVENTEEN   self-discipline, though possibly with an illusion of grace without effort. Patriarchal magic is also indicated — the mystical key in the context of over-structured decimal consciousness. Yet seventeen will successfully take us into the New Age, as the eight it contains is the realism which grounds this energy in the now.

EIGHTEEN   strong moon sense, as nine is the prime moon number which is emphasized here. An intense spirituality and ethical or moral awareness which experience growth and activity, and progress with eighteen.

NINETEEN   the length of a complete lunar-solar cycle, nineteen indicates the self-expression of an integrated individual.

TWENTY   the self and the universe — together or at odds? This is the number of the individual taking responsibility for herself in the world. How do you judge your life?

TWENTY-ONE   the sisterhood meets magic. The number of successful personal choice and matured magical ability.

NOUGHT   the circle of wholeness. The completion of 'just being' without the need to add anything to the experience. The primeval void, the abyss of beginning. All knowing is expressed in this figure.

SYMBOLS

Symbols persist throughout all of life, making dynamic patterns which create harmony. Nature forms symbols in plants, animal behaviour, seasonal synchronicity, genetic coding, everywhere. We create additional symbols in our minds and give these expression in our social life. The decline of spiritual awareness over the last eight thousand years has meant that knowledge of the meaning, inherent power and ways to influence these symbolic forms has been lost. Recently attempts have been made at reinterpretation by psychologists, suggesting archetypes and a collective unconscious. Psychical researchers of the same period posit the Group Mind and similar explanations. These efforts are evidence that the music of the spheres is once again becoming audible and people are beginning to grope for a language in which to communicate with one another about it.

Tarot cards are one such means of communication. Each throw, each new spread, captures an energy pattern, the harmony of the moment known in the east as the Tao, and makes it visible for study and interpretation. As extra words only scatter the power and make it harder to discern meaning, Tarot facilitates reduction of the ego and disciplined containment of personality in the reader, thus avoiding some of the most dangerous pitfalls of psychology. For this reason, the cards are an excellent tool for real change as they enable us to see into the world of truth to which our ordinary perception blinds us.

We must reclaim symbols and reinterpret them in light of our current knowledge. Those disciplined in the occult sciences and in the habit of a daily meditation will be aware of the shifting mists. We may share an impatience with ignorant romantics, who are unable to distinguish which of their responses are natural from those that are only strongly conditioned. The underlying silver cord of continuity is FAITH IN WOMYN as channels of goddess love in the world.

The Tarot is rich in symbolic imagery. Many well-known symbols occur throughout the pack. The ankh, the sign of life in Egypt, is a version of the modern women's symbol. Represented by an oval atop a T-cross, when appearing as the glyph for Venus this symbol will have a slightly rounder head and a lower crossbar. The infinity symbol, the eight lying on its side, — often called a lemniscate — also occurs frequently, and is of Eastern as well as Western significance, appearing as it does in ritual Hindu dance patterns. Wings are used in cruder Tarot packs to denote the spiritual essence of the life form depicted. Rainbows indicate the mutuality of heaven and earth, the co-operation of the worlds in creating love.
Animals also have symbolic significance. Horses represent the dragon come to earth, the goddess Epona, Rhiannon, mare-Demeter whose mane represents strength and fertility, who rides the wind and whispers secrets. The pair of cow's horns containing the full moon is a symbol of goddess adoration, the cow goddess of ancient Babylon being represented in this sigil which usually appears as a headdress. The Tau cross entwined by two snakes is called a Caduceus and is the sign of healing adopted from the healing goddesses by Hippocrates, the so-called father of modern medicine. Snakes or serpents symbolize wisdom, dragons represent the creative live force. One of these creatures swallowing its own tail means eternal life. It is said that when a serpent swallows a serpent it becomes a dragon, a symbolic statement of the creative power of lesbian lovemaking. Dion Fortune, a modern Qabalist who was a member of the Golden Dawn believes that snakes also signify initiation. Pigs are special to goddess, especially three-colour pigs. Dogs, too, belong to goddess, and often stand near pairs of pillars guarding the entrance, as the Dog of Langport guards

the entrance to the Glastonbury Zodiac.

The moon represents intuition, emotional energy and mystical self-knowledge. A new crescent shows powers that will grow, while a waxing moon shows consolidation. The moon moves rapidly through the zodiac each month and so shows changeability, even moodiness. Being dazzled by reflections on the surface of the water can distract the querent from seeking the hidden depths. Trees represent life and goddess, two energies that cannot be separated from one another. Each type of tree represents a particular aspect of her creativity. Similarly pillars, either singly or in pairs, represent the universal mother. A single feather, usually white, traditionally denotes truth. Yellow indicates spiritual and intellectual stimulation. Green is the colour of harmony and is traditionally associated with the heart chakra.

In learning to recognize symbols, and in developing your own language for interpretation, wide ranging study will be of immense value. Read books, visit museums, look at pictures and spend time in the country. Freeing up your intuition and psychic perception is another invaluable aspect of learning symbol-language. Listen to your inner voice, look with your third eye, be aware of your dreams and take note of your bodily sensations. In this way each of us will come to her own understanding of symbols, and the rich diversity of womyn's wisdom will indeed be a source of our strength.

THE NUMBERS IN THE MAJOR ARCANA : KEY WORDS

I   ALIVENESS

II   RECEPTIVITY

III   INTEGRATION

IV   UNIFICATION

V   DETERMINATION

VI   CREATIVITY

VII   KNOWLEDGE

VIII	POTENCY
IX	THE THIRD EYE
X	KARMA
XI	THE INNER LIGHT
XII	COMMUNICATION
XIII	DROWNING
XIV	DISSOLUTION
XV	PERPETUAL CHANGE
XVI	STRENGTHENING LIMITS
XVII	THE POWER OF THOUGHT
XVIII	WATERS OF LIFE
XIX	SUCCESSFUL IDEALISM
XX	REGENERATION
XXI	FULFILLED CREATION
O	MEANING

I   THE ALCHEMIST (MAGICIAN)   Fire

The Alchemist or Magician is the first card of the Major Arcana.
The Aries card, the Alchemist represents an untried individual,
one whose ability has not yet been tempered by experience.
With this card, an individual arrives in the world with the spirit
necessary to make her mark, the drive to carve out her space,
the energy to determine her own world. This individual is
capable of creating herself by shaping the four elements
according to her will. An ingenious individual, the Alchemist
rises to every challenge, not yet able to discriminate.
Consequently her fire burns and flashes, her energy is rashly
used and her heat is often kindled by the arrogance of pride.

A forceful personality, the querent with this card may be
impetuous, often launching projects she has no real interest in
completing. Similarly, the discovery of the querent's abilities in

ritual magic may be enjoyed for their own sake, as an egotistical experience of power, without being linked to a spiritual direction or ethical philosophy. The querent has not yet considered the other forces which help to create her talents, and she thinks herself omnipotent. A querent with this card has a lot of intense energy which can be very influential in her environment. Though she is likely always to have been aware of this force within her, the querent may still be seeking channels for its expression. Responsibility in this endeavour will be her best protection against accident. Her innocence will protect her only so long as it lasts. She must realize that ingenuousness, however attractive, will not lend acceptability to selfishness or cruelty.

The card of Brigit, Keeper of the Fire, mistress of poetry, healing and smithcraft, this card can indicate the ability of the querent to transform a difficult situation through the insistence of her charm. It is a card of personality and charisma. Psychic ability is likely to be indicated. Traditionally this card represents the maker of calendars, an individual with the sagacity to define the temporal reality of society.

II   THE INITIATE (PRIESTESS)   Water

The Initiate, second card of the Major Arcana, is the intuitive, inwardlooking aspect of one's character. Here, the emotions present themselves to our awareness and we have the first opportunity to know ourselves and to become aware of our spiritual potential. I also call this card the Neophyte, a new initiate who studies to further her understanding as well as working with her inner energies to enhance her perception. For only by combining intuitive insight and revelation with reason and disciplined study can we be truly integrated and restore sanity to the world.

A card of the new moon, growth and development are indicated here. Another name for this card is The Gatekeeper, for, if you can give her the correct password, she will help you move through the veils to approach the deeper mysteries. Sitting at the mouth of the cave, the Initiate is the guardian of the maze. This individual is learning the art of silence, in which her inner voice can speak to her with moral clarity. This is the card of Rahab, prophetic Hebrew goddess of the sea.

In the creation of ourselves this aspect is very important to our womon-wise ways of dealing with life. The only water card in the first loop of the lemniscate, it is essential that this quality is not neglected. The Priestess is not insistent or demanding; we must seek her out if we wish to learn the lessons she can teach. In looking for her in our lives we are taking the first step in our spiritual development in our current incarnation. Consciously seeking our path, desiring to locate the gatekeeper, is the willingness that is needed to bring us into tune with the cosmic rhythms that can guide us as we progress.

When poorly aspected, this card may indicate an over-sensitivity to emotional or psychic influences which can pull the querent off her centre. The card of Pisces, potential to be a good medium with clairvoyant ability is shown here. The querent must remember that she is at the beginning stage of her development and not neglect her study or her meditation if she is to go deeper in her knowledge. If this card is inverted the querent may be out of touch with her feelings, or have a tendency to self-sacrifice rather than true service.

III LOVE   Air

The crisis in the world today is about the quality of life and Card Three reminds us that Love maintains the fabric of existence. Three is the number of connection and this Gemini card shows that the querent is in touch with the energies around her. Able to feel the life-giving stimulus in the atmosphere, when she is centred she can use this power alchemically to generate change. The querent's awareness of the healing power of love in the universe makes her able to be a channel for its expression by the way she lives her life. Thus, she is taking personal responsibility for ending suffering and so is one of those who can help to save the world. Any who can are being called upon now, even if we feel we are not ready. The Love card is a reminder of this work. Look for and give expression to the love which is all around and it will come back to you increased.

This card is called the choice card. How we choose to learn the lessons of love in this life will strongly influence our personal experience and future karma. If the querent is pulled by contradictory forces, desire for emotional and spiritual love may conflict. Love is the alchemical catalyst necessary to create the sense of wholeness we need to survive. It is important not to mistake the burning flames of passion or the watery yearnings of desire for spiritual longing for the spacious dignity of non-possessive compassionate love. If the querent is involved in a relationship, extra awareness is required to keep love alive. The card of Cardea, later the goddess Flora, the wind whispers her message of love as an inspiration to all who listen in a sacred grove. Let the vitality of this energy teach you of love.

When poorly aspected, this card may show a man coming between two women or the patriarchal institution of giving women to slavery in marriage. Though we are taught to believe such unions are contitioned by love, they too often become imprisonment, particularly when held by vows in the church of a masculist god. When inverted, this card may indicate the dissolution of a legal marriage.

IV THE ELDER   Earth

The Elder is a card of worldly authority deriving from knowledge of social custom, and this individual holds sway because of her experience. She is able to heal social divisions due to her familiarity with society's traditions. Depicted in the Egyptian Gypsies Tarot as a woman holding a Tau cross spiralled round by two snakes, this caduceus indicates the healing powers of someone wise in the ways of the group and skilled at binding together. As the first earth card of the Major Arcana, the Elder represents a rooting of the self in the practical realities of life.

This card indicates a stable and harmonious relationship with the material forces of society. The querent's popularity as a leader is founded on her reputation for prudence, one of the four cardinal virtues of medieval times. The individual here is involved with public life and has worldly authority; she may be concerned with institutions or systems of rule. The goddess Sal-ma, for whom palm leaves are waved in honour, is indicated by this card.

In early patriarchal times women had to dress as men in order to retain social authority, as in the church men had to dress as wimmin to usurp spiritual leadership. P.C. Smith indicates this phenomenon of cross-dressing in her depiction of The Emperor. In that sense the card is concerned with the material power to oppress: brute force, conquering nature, prisons and armies.

The Capricorn card, when detrimentally aspected, can indicate an individual who is excessively structured in her approach and is unable to move with the tides of change. Such persons are preoccupied with maintaining their power and are often unable to believe in the importance of any reality other than the worldly one.

V THE CHARIOT (SELF-DISCIPLINE)   Fire

The Chariot or Self-Discipline is the second Major Arcana card to represent will. The querent has created herself through each of the four elements and is now ready to assert herself. Her will has been harnessed, her intention focused, and this concentrated energy can drive her in her chosen direction. When the will has united the personality, the ego, and the spirit, the Self can move directly to realization. The left and right brains are integrated in understanding and desire, enabling the querent to proceed unhindered toward her immediate goal. If however the querent's intentions are divided she may remain static, held by pulls in conflicting directions. In this case she will do two or more things with limited success.

It is possible the querent may have a law suit to go through. If she is carrying too much structure her progress will be impeded. Similarly, if the disparate elements of her personality have been brought together too forcibly the concerted effort may lack harmony. In an unevolved subject this card can represent vengeance.

This card has also been called Victory or The Conqueror. In the Qabalist tradition Yaweh is seen seated in a chariot, the image freqently depicted in this card. To the Druids this card belongs to Awen, and is represented by an arrow. In the Dianic tradition the goddess Rhiannon, a form of the horse goddess associated with the autumn equinox, is indicated here. The Chariot is the card of Sagittarius and may indicate travel by car, train, plane or space ship.

VI THE MATRIARCH   Earth

The Matriarch indicates harmonious progress in the development of one's relationship with the earth forces. The Matriarch derives her earthly authority from her creative and bountiful association with the forces of nature. At home in the material world she is capable of relaxed and benevolent rulership. She feels the earth vibrations and uses Feng Shui or geomancy to keep her energies in tune with the dragon. A strong presence, she is tenacious and others may come to her for protection and guidance.

This card shows the ability to create something material and potentially lasting outside oneself. This can mean artistic creativity or social reliability, the Matriarch providing energy to maintain social institutions. Juno, or Siri, the goddess of luck and plenty is represented here. This card may show someone involved with the growth movement or indicate successful pathworkings.

When detrimentally aspected, this Taurus card indicates someone who over-indulges in sensual pleasure, who squanders her creative energy in a constant orgy of manifestation. Unable to discipline herself, she takes pride in her beauty and is continually showing off. She may complement her vanity with laziness, and have bureaucratic tendencies.

VII THE KEEPER OF THE MYSTERIES
(THE PROPHET)   Air

The Keeper of the Mysteries or the Prophet is Card Seven of
the Major Arcana. This magical card of revelation is the Air
Dragon, the card of Uranus. The Tarot pack contains a dragon
in each element and this dragon of the mind is the only one to
appear in the first portion of the lemniscate. The road to
wisdom may be entered upon if one can understand the
messages this card conveys.

The true Priestess of the deck, the goddess Pythia reveals
the secrets to Rahab, offering spiritual guidance to the querent
who is creating herself. Also known as The Paragon or The
Kahuna, this individual incarnates moral wisdom in her daily
life and is often a reliable teacher. The querent here has made
some progress in this or other lives in her discernment of occult
knowledge and her ability to comprehend esoteric matters.
She can hear and understand the wind as she howls and
whispers, cries and sighs round the cycles of the year. Because
she is prepared to be responsible with her knowledge the
querent is now being given the keys to the hidden mysteries,
the unseen realms.

When negatively aspected, this card can represent the
hierarchical authoritarian church, and a clinging to ritual form
without deciphering its spiritual content. The potential
dogmatism of misused air powers is great; as H. P. Blavatsky
reminds us: "Intellect is the greatest slayer of the real." The
other weakness with this intense card is superstition, a danger
likely to come to the fore unless the true nature of seven in the
New Age is comprehended. The querent may be in danger of
developing a messiah complex, and unnecessarily mystifying
the wisdom she has to share.

VIII STRENGTH (COURAGE)   Earth

Strength represents courage and power in the material world
and shows the fulfilled relationship of the querent with her
environment. The harmony she has achieved allows her to
influence the earth energies. At home with nature, she is able
to integrate with the unseen forces to manifest that which she
desires. Her vital energy is very forceful. Also known as
Fortitude, another of the medieval cardinal virtues, the querent
here has the self-discipline to persevere, knowing she is on the
most fruitful path for her personal evolution and that the work
she is doing will increase her alchemical intensity.

Cybele, Queen of Summer, is shown here. The lion and
the bumblebee are special to her, as is the oak, all being
symbols of immense strength and beauty. It is also claimed that

the sphinx represents Cybele — a creature composed of lion, womon, eagle and cow, all sacred to goddess. A querent aware of her power in the world will now have the courage to use it with calmness and clear intention. As with all the cards there is a danger here of egotism, or working only for her own personal goals. Another name for this card is The Enchantress.

6. Major Arcana Card VIII — Strength

The card of Venus, this querent will enjoy sensuality and know how to give herself pleasuring experiences. There is a legend that Venusians colonized Earth and it is certain that the relationship of Venus and Gaea is a fertile one. This is a card of optimisim. Because of the querent's skill in taming the alchemical lion she must use her ability to bewitch with care and guard against possessiveness.

IX   JUSTICE (THE TRUTH)   Air

Justice, a cardinal virtue, is represented by the goddess Parthenos, protectress of those who create themselves with conscious awareness. This card is about accepting responsibility for truth and so is also associated with the Egyptian goddess Maat. With the clear vision of the third eye, this individual is able to perceive reality directly and to proclaim the natural laws of harmony. Thus the querent with the card is the lawgiver, the dispenser of justice.

It is important that her vision be tempered by mercy, taking into account how people really are as well as the ideal state to which we may attain. The upturned sword representing mercy and compassion is a reminder of this need. Without these qualities the querent will find herself isolated by her unforgivingness. Similarly, if she is harsh in her opinions, such harshness will come back to her. It may be helpful to meditate on QuanYin, Buddhist goddess of mercy, when considering this card.

This is the card of Libra and indicates that the querent should strive for mental integration or balance, being aware that an excess of mental activity can be difficult to discipline, or even to recognize. The mental energy of our culture has meant that the essence signified here succeeded the Earth Mother at Delphi as the transition was made from earth to sky. At that time a distortion of relationships occurred which has never been corrected. The sensitivity of this querent's astuteness may enable her to restore harmony to the interaction of the elements.

There is also a danger of superficiality with this card, an appearance of calm and control which belies a turbulent interior. The power inherent in the role of law-giver can be very corrupting. Only by remembering that you are giving birth to yourself through your efforts can accepting the responsibility for truth be a humbling and liberating experience.

With this clear vision the individual is now ready to take another turn on the spiral of her evolution, into the next portion of the lemniscate.

X   WHEEL OF FORTUNE   Fire

The Wheel is the driving energy of our lives. Sometimes referred to as karma, or as fate, this force propels us along the path we have determined for ourselves by our actions. Every day we shape our own future, focusing on some possibilities and dimming the chances of other occurrences by the way we use our power. When this card appears in a spread the querent is turning another corner in her life, travelling on the spiral of her evolution. As its number ten shows, the querent's life is now over-full; the potential of the moment — the present situation — has been realized and she is moving into a new life space.

As with retrograde planets, there may be times when it appears your life is going backwards, but you are always being presented with opportunities to learn and to develop, and never precisely repeat the same experience twice. The card of

Mars, the Wheel represents the source of cosmic compulsion in our lives. Try to learn the lessons hidden in this change.

This card is said in Hindu and Buddhist mythology to belong to the goddess Kali — The Destroyer, whose age, through which we are now living, will last a full 423,000 years. This card has also been called the spiral of life, and the circle of time. In the Dianic tradition the goddess Trivia, Ruler of the Crossroads, is represented here.

The change indicated by this card can mean a disruption of lifestyle, and the querent may be tempted to abandon responsibility for the direction her life is taking. It is important to remember that we create our own lives and learn the most by being responsible for our own experience. Conscious determination will create the path of deepest meaning and widest fulfillment.

XI   THE WISE WOMON (THE GEOMANCER)   Earth

Her lantern in the shape of an hour glass, her light an eight-pointed star, this card shows Diana measuring the seasons and maintaining eco-harmony in the world. Eleven is the number of the Tao. A geomancer, the individual here seeks to find the meaning of this earthly incarnation. Green Tara, the Bodhisattva of Compassion, may help her to chart the dragon path. In seeking her relationship with the cosmos the querent will develop her concentration in solitude and will learn to read new meanings in the signs and omens of the world. She will be exact and cautious in her interpretation of symbols. Her attributes are compassion and silence.

The first card in the second portion of the lemniscate, this individual knows herself, and has found the source of her inner light. Though she keeps it shrouded in mystery, she is prepared to help light the way for other true seekers. The Virgo card, this querent is 'unto herself' as were the temple virgins of older times, and is not frivolous in dispensing her light and power. A querent with this card recognizes the importance of finding and holding her own centre. An oracle, or going to consult an oracle, may also be indicated.

This card can also represent the influence of retrograde planets on the querent and may mean she is unable to see the wood for the trees in her search for herself. A querent with this card often needs to be reminded that the inner journey, long and lonely though it is, brings inner peace through self-realization and that such work is in service of the universal mother. Every woman with the courage to find and meet herself will strengthen the presence of goddess in the world.

When negatively indicated, this card can mean a querent

who is obsessive about detail or selfishly involved with her own development to the exclusion of life around her. The deceit of arrogance may have led the querent to believe she can guide others before she knows herself. If any of the patriarchal religious institutions are indicated the querent can expect to meet with hypocrisy and falsehood, corruption and betrayal.

XII   HANGING (HEALING)   Air
This card represents the serenity and health that come with an inner psychic twist. The new perspective afforded by this experience of sudden insight yields immediate beatitude, a compassionate joy that radiates healing energy throughout the querent's life.

Though traditionally seen as the card of sacrifice, the collapse of materialism and male dominance now occurring will help us understand the error of that interpretation. The yearly demise of the god Osiris was, in reality, the return of the Messenger Goddess Iris to the underworld through the Os, the mouth of the abyss. Thus, the cyclically returning season of lamentation and the transforming powers of Mercury are represented by this card. Belief in the power of truth to support you in your life is the vision vouchsafed here, and this card indicates the querent's trust. Symbolizing the maker of alphabets, this is the doorway to the runes. Artemis Caryatis, goddess of inspiration and healing, guards the entrance.

When negatively aspected, this card can represent immobilization, the Bliss Trap that prevents the querent taking action to change any of the oppressive conditions in her life.

XIII   DEATH (CHANGE)   Water
Death, Card Thirteen, represents deep personal transformation. It is necessary to die to be reborn. The extent of the transformation will be determined by the querent's willingness to change, and she must look within herself to find her true intention.

Symbolically this card represents a return to the true source of power in the watery depths of primordial chaos. The universal mother who creates all life is the primeval void to which all form returns. This image, and the number associated with it here, have received and held most of the fears of patriarchy. Goddess-loving womyn will have to free ourselves from the bondage of masculist thought before we can willingly drink the wine of life through the energies of this card.

This card rarely means a physical death and the reader should look for many other signs, both in the cards and in her psychic sensations, before she gives such an interpretation. A clearing away of the debris of an out-worn mode of existence is the experience usually indicated, and the querent may feel she is being stripped bare of her pretensions. This often unexpected change resulting from prevailing circumstances is likely to leave the querent purified, cleansed in preparation for her new life.

The watery hag, this card represents a sea serpent and is the Water Dragon of the Tarot. It is associated with Pluto, and the goddess Sedna, Eskimo Queen of the Sea Beasts. In Celtic mythology this card belongs to the Moirae, or Fates, and recollects the querent's responsibility in shaping her own destiny.

XIV   THE THUNDERBOLT/THE LIGHTNING FLASH
Fire

Card Fourteen is the Fire Dragon. Usually known as the Lightning Struck Tower, Prison or House of God, I prefer to call it The Thunderbolt or The Lightning Flash. For the fire from heaven illuminates, allowing us to perceive reality directly. This card represents the fire in the rain, the release of the creative power of the spirit within the environment created by the querent's intuition. The querent's understanding of the social order, its character and her place in it, are blasted by her own awareness. Occasionally represented by the neolithic double axe used to behead kings, this card is sometimes called The Volcano to remind us that we bring about this experience by our own volition and must not think of ourselves as victimized by it.

The defeat of the ruling order shatters conditioned beliefs about social structures which have been imprisoning the querent's spirit. The querent may have become suddenly aware of the falseness of patriarchal society. Whether this experience is a catharsis or a devastation depends on the querent. Those in their ivory towers will be sent crashing to the ground, and latent psychic powers will be released. Prana is described as being 'like lightning' and a querent meeting this card should expect a jolt. This sudden realization will remind us of the transience of material existence and give the querent a taste of enlightenment. Such dramatic moments of illumination are necessary to clear away obstacles to the creation of a new way of life. Neptune, attributed to this card, brings revelation through experience. The goddess Tina, armed with the triple thunderbolt or trident, is represented here.

When badly aspected, the querent is consciously resisting the forces of her own development and is making this experience harsh and frightening by not preparing herself. This could mean she is clinging to outmoded structures in a desperate search for security or in order to maintain her status in a hierarchy. There are big changes due for the world — some call it a Great Purification — and those who do not willingly move with the times may well be blasted out of their complacency.

XV TEMPERANCE   Water

Temperance, Card Fifteen, represents Time the Eternal Alchemist. As number fifteen, she is the fulcrum or centre point of the far edge of the lemniscate and bears this power and responsibility with ease. This card reminds us that change is the law of nature, and that all elements are transmuted through the action of Time. Iris, Goddess of the Rainbow, Messenger of the Heavens, is shown mixing the waters of perception. Temperance is the only medieval cardinal virtue to appear in the latter portion of the lemniscate. The other lessons having been learnt earlier in one's spiritual evolution, developing a temperate character follows many of life's formative experiences and prepares us for the culminating stages of self-creation.

Moving in harmony with Time, this querent feels herself fully integrated with the Now and empowered by the deep resonance such synchronicity creates in her life. A querent with this card is likely to feel she has at last caught up with herself and that time is 'on her side'. The card of Jupiter, and associated too with the cauldron of Cerridwen, there is an expansiveness here which can encourage optimism in the querent. Her higher mind will be receptive to wider meanings and beginning to understand the timelessness of existence. The querent may feel herself learning the art of patience. The freeing of the querent's creative imagination will help her to feel reconciled with the movement of the waves of energy which are the tides of life. 'Everything she touches she changes, everything she changes she touches.'

When poorly aspected, this card can show a querent who is at odds with Time, trying to accomplish things for which there is no real impetus. She may also be frustrated in her attempts to understand the unifying forces of life, and feel doomed to endless struggle.

XVI THE EARTH DRAGON   Earth

The Earth Dragon is very significant, especially to those who practise the Dianic Craft. For reclaiming physical existence as an essential aspect of our spiritual being is a contribution feminist witches are making to a new understanding of reality. Only by achieving such integration can we hope to save the planet from destruction and so enable life on earth to continue. Sensitivity to earth energies will help us to be grounded and aware of the inherent limitations we must accept for survival.

When we cease hiding our bodily realities and come to love them and to accept the beauty of their demands, we will no longer be enslaved. Then we will be truly able to regulate our passions so that we retain a zest for life without letting our appetites knock us about. Pleasure is an essential aspect of aliveness, but the intensity of passion needs to be channelled. By vibrating together with our sisters Gaea, Luna and Grainne we can integrate ourselves into the music of the spheres and so ensure realism on earth. This card also reminds us that it is possible to spare ourselves the wasted energy of struggling against inevitable restrictions.

The goddess of this card is Marpessa, the old sow who rules midwinter, as does Saturn, the planet of this card. Also attributed to BonaDea, this good goddess would prophesy only for wimmin. In a mixed pantheon this card is also assigned to Pan, The Curious One. Some would have us call this card the devil. But as Sybil Leek reminds us: 'Reincarnation teaches that everyone must tread her own karmic path and does not acknowledge the existence of a devil. This is regarded as one's own ignorance, greed and stupidity.'

XVII   THE STAR   Air
The Star of Hope signifies the New Age we are now entering and represents true individualism, the fearlessness of the querent to go naked in the world, without the cloak of her personality to shield her. Looking back to the watery Age of self-denying Pisces just ending, and forward to the practical Capricornian Age to come, the Aquarian bridges the gap and represents the spiritual cleansing of the people through the knowledge we will gain.

Hathor, Queen of Heaven, is the cow goddess. In this Age the occult sciences will become common study and esoteric understanding will be widespread. With this new vision, a commitment to honour Gaea will arise. Heaven and earth will be united again by the determination of the people. The querent has the opportunity to move in harmony with the energy of these times. If she is a sensitive being she will be able to respond to the heavenly guidance being poured out upon the earth and its inhabitants.

This card should show eight eight-pointed stars. Crowley, and others following his lead, show seven-pointed stars.

Though seven is a key number in Western mysticism, it is only in a moral/spiritual context that this power becomes meaningful. Seven is the number of magic, eight of application, developing skill and apprenticeship. By applying the wisdom gained in service of the guiding principles of this Age one will truly become an avatar.

The eight-pointed star is also a symbol of Islam, the patriarchal religion rising to dominance at this time. Hathor is remembered in the Muslim world in the hand of Fatima, often made with cow-like features. Here we can learn some of the dangers that may befall the querent — a denial of her creative power, accepting submission and servitude within the patriarchy, a belief in her soullessness which feeds a sense of futility. The New Age also invites an excessive individualism and opportunism, an exploiting of the openings provided by these changing times to enhance one's personal fortunes without concern for community or for Gaea. Yet the clarity of vision of this New Age will proclaim its inevitability even if the querent is unable to join in the celebration of new life. This card can show that you are trying to sort out your relationship to the new age, and its placing in a spread will be particularly important in reading this card.

XVIII THE MOON   Water

The moon is the mirror of the soul and this is the card of deep self-knowing. In our current solar age, with its emphasis on burning light, it has become difficult to appreciate the true characteristics of the moon. Her light is cool and accepting. She demands no sacrifices, nor is her light insisting or perpetual. The dark moon allows us periods of privacy, times of inward examination. Other moons cast shadows which allow an exploration of potential in a variety of forms and encourage the imagination.

Whether full or dark or somewhere in between, the invisible influence of the moon on our tides and cycles is continual. Not only does she direct the watery tides; air currents too respond to her pull. This explains the close relationship between mysticism and the occult, intuition and inspiration, and reminds us of the intimate connection of the earth and the heavenly bodies.

The full moon is well-known to have a strong magnetic effect which brings out hidden emotions. These experiences can help us to achieve a deeper self-awareness, though when uncontrolled the passion of our inner fire can lead to self-destruction. Our character and aspirations will determine whether we use the shadow light to deceive. This card

THE MAJOR ARCANA   89

represents a major opportunity for growth and an individual
with the resolve to face herself will make creative use of this
experience.

A prime weakness to be aware of with this card is
excessive emotionalism. In this state the querent flounders in
her own watery depths, confused by her own self-deception
and a tendency to escape into fantasy. These sources of
confusion may be habitual patterns of response in her life.
Another weakness represented by this card is an inclination to
be superstitious. Fear of shadows, part of the dogma of solar
patriarchy, creates a failure of nerve or lack of confidence that
can lead to an over-empowering of external forces, giving
moonlight a glamourized hypnotic power over your
consciousness. Such a querent is likely to be misled by
reflections on the surface, and fail to plumb the depths. A
querent who is vulnerable to these difficulties may need
counselling and a physical regimen to develop robust health,
and should also be reminded that she can reclaim power over
her inner self through a regular practice of meditation. In this
way she can find a harmony with her water cycles, and
experience a periodic cleansing in the pure waters of womon
wisdom. A querent with this card must accept the changeability
of her feelings and trust that beneath these fluctuations she is
developing a clearer awareness of her true nature.

The card of Cancer, traditionally the goddess Luna, the
Dianic tradition also recognizes the African goddess Mawu in
the moon.

XIX   THE SUN   Fire
There are three creation myths about the sun and the moon.
The sun is usually spoken of as the daughter of the moon.
Occasionally, however, they are recognized as sisters and
according to some legends the sun and the moon are lesbian
lovers who parthenogenically create the earth. The number of
this card, nineteen, is the length of years of a complete
moon-sun cycle of relationship. Thus the astrological wisdom
of the Tarot and the interwoven matrices of meaning are again
revealed. Called Arinna in Anatolia and Amaterasu by the
Shinto in Japan, the Celtic Sun Goddess is known as Grainne
or Greine. The card of Leo, an evolved querent can use the
energy of this card to express her spirit. The Sun, being one of
the last cards in the Major Arcana series, represents the
developed or 'perfected' personality. People getting this card
have sufficiently integrated themselves so as to be able to
achieve success.

Sometimes success is achieved by containing our power

within ourselves, and letting only our gentler rays of light shine, as the sun does in the spring and autumn. The I Ching speaks of these situations in hexagrams such as The Preponderance of the Small. At other times the situation may call for the full force of our personal influence when, like the August sunshine, we must be as constant and enduring as possible in our efforts. We must also not forget the winter season of hibernation when the sun is just warm enough to sustain life, and does not display herself. So, when you are interpreting this card for someone, remember that success takes many forms. Someone who is experiencing a period of introversion may nonetheless be using her personality in the most effective way, helping herself to be successful in her efforts.

7. Major Arcana Card XIX — The Sun

In some Tarot packs there are two humun figures in this card but the more usual image of one figure is a reflection of the extreme individualization which has occurred in our time. Thus, The Sun can represent the patriarchal development of nuclear power, the denial of the importance of the moon in daily life and the searing force of blind fire, which destroys all it touches in an orgy of self-satisfying dominance. Use your intuition when reading this card to discover whether the querent is being too pushy, greedy and insensitive in the situation in which she is seeking success and, if necessary, remind her of the need for seasonal rhythms. Each of us has our own cycle of seasons; these may be longer or shorter than agricultural ones and may or may not occur at the same time as those in nature. Success comes more easily and is more enduring when we express our selves in harmony with the natural rhythms of our existence.

XX JUDGEMENT
(SPIRITUAL REAWAKENING)   Water

The Judgement card is a card of spiritual reawakening and can indicate that the querent is preparing herself to meet the challenge that is coming to the world. Frequently depicting an angel calling from heaven, this card should show the universal creative force touching the querent's inner being, as it does in the Mexican Tarot which portrays a serpent descending and is called 'Crisis'. A water card, this force reaches us through music. A meditation practice which includes chanting will help awaken your inner ear to the vibrations of this spiritual sound. The Mesopotamian goddess Nammu — the Sea, Creator of Life, is associated with this card.

The illustration of this card in successive decks shows the increasing privatization and separation that has accompanied the development of our individuality in the last few hundred years. From the group of people in a shared sea of existence depicted in some decks, this card in the P. C. Smith design presents individuals in self-contained boxes. The truth of her vision is in the unwelcoming attitude of the man to the message from heaven. In the coming Age we will experience true individuation without false consciousness alienating us and destroying community.

The card of Scorpio, the querent's karma is revealing itself to her now in this life, and her spiritual potential is being realized. If she has denied the call of her inner voice and refused the inner journey, the judgement is for her to suffer her emotions, a slave to her fears and desires without the stability of spiritual awareness, sometimes called faith, as a personal source of reassurance. If you cling to negativity and suffering you shall bring yourself to suffering again and again.

When poorly aspected, this card may indicate a fanatical querent, one who adamantly denies her spirituality or who is immersed in religious zealousness. Her past vindictiveness to others may be rebounding on her. The querent must judge each situation in which she finds herself to determine whether it assists her growth and, if so, how to derive the most benefit from it. If this card appears repeatedly for a querent the question of her spiritual regeneration is being presented to her for her judgement. Selfish choice will bring hardship, but the decision is hers. The commitment to awaken to spiritual life will create a new future for the querent.

XXI   THE WORLD

The World shows a fully created individual, one who is now aware of herself as an incarnated being on this earth. All the elements are available to her and she senses her ability to do anything she chooses. Achaiva The Spinner, a form of Demeter, is associated with this card, reminding the querent of her capacity to shape her own reality from the threads of her own being.

This querent has not made a choice nor focused her energy. She is still celebrating the dance of life and glorying in her creative potential. While unquestionably a joyous state of self-awareness, such a situation, if allowed to continue too long, will dissipate the querent's energy.

This card indicates specifically the querent's spiritual evolution, as the four elements illustrated in the corners by images of the fixed signs makes us aware. Though doubly developed since her beginnings as The Alchemist, she is avoiding commitment. The querent here has the immediate possibility of realizing her potential. The use or otherwise that she makes of this opportunity will shape her future. Thus the querent's choice of life activity will be most fortunate if it nourishes the needs of her inner being.

O   THE FOOL

The Fool is the strongest card in the entire Tarot pack, and is generally seen to constitute a section of its own. Containing all four elements and symbolizing the questing spirit, the number of the Fool is nought. The circle of wholeness, image of the world egg, representing the primal void from which comes all form, the Fool reminds us of the spiral momentum of evolution. This card represents the quest for Truth, the inner journey, the path of life. An individual with this card will be protected by her innocence as she travels through life, until she has eaten of the tree of life sufficiently. From then on her protection will come from her acceptance of responsibility. Only if she demands knowledge and refuses responsibility will misfortune result. It is important not to confuse laziness with innocence. Chance occurrence due to undeveloped attention is not a guarantee of safety. Each querent will make of this card what her own inner being is capable of comprehending.

The Fool, also known as The Juggler, can represent

madness, an individual so distracted by the contradictions of existence that she can no longer define her own reality. This querent is buffetted by the forces around her, at the mercy of the tides of energy in which she is immersed. Frequently, it is only faith in life itself that can keep such a querent from suicide.

Foolishness is another possible attribute of this card. A querent who is oblivious to the forces in her environment may meet with unexpected mishaps. Only when fully aware and harmonized with the energies of the cosmos as they express themselves in a particular life can an individual move unimpeded on her path, freed of the likelihood of foolish error.

Optimistic faith is the keynote of the Fool, and the querent with this card is likely to have a deep and abiding belief in the creative potential of life, including her own. She trusts in the universe to sustain her.

CHAPTER FIVE
THE SPREADS

THE SPREADS AVAILABLE

The Eighteen-Card Gypsy Method

The Lunar Cross

The Stone Circle

The Zodiac Spread

The Thirteen Card Pyramid

The Twenty-One Card Pyramid

The Solar Cross

The Seven Card Key

The Horseshoe Spread

NOTES ON CARD POSITION

In general the cards are laid by the reader beginning at the edge of the cloth nearest to her. Thus, for most spreads, card one is at the reader's side of the cloth while the top of the spread, where the significators are placed, is nearest the querent. With the Lunar Cross, card one is on the querent's side and card seven is nearest the reader; with the Solar Cross, card four rather than card one is nearest the reader.

Inverted cards are determined by their relationship to the reader, not the querent. I place significators inverted to me, upright to the querent, on the querent's side of the table, except with the Horseshoe Spread and the Zodiac Spread where the significators are placed in the centre of the circle. As these cards specifically represent her, and are the first ones read, these procedures help the querent focus her attention and tune in to the psychic energies being generated.

In all the diagrams the significators are designated 'S', 'S_1', or 'S_2'.

THE EIGHTEEN CARD GYPSY METHOD

This spread is used to reveal the querent's general life patterns and is read without significators. The cards are cooked, shuffled, cut and laid as described. Begin by turning up the bottom row of cards (numbers one to six). These cards represent the underlying energies in the querent's life, her past, the roots of her development and in alchemical terms the base elements of her character. Then turn up the middle row and read these sequentially (seven through twelve). This row represents the forces in her life that the querent is consciously able to command, her 'adult' or rational self, and the challenges she is currently facing. Begin also to look for relationships between cards one/two and seven/eight, three/four and nine/ten, five/six and eleven/twelve but do not comment on these yet. Now turn up the top line and read cards thirteen to eighteen in turn. This row represents the potential energies available to the querent, the likely outcome of her efforts, the possibilitites for her spiritual evolution, and her future direction. When you have examined the cards in this way, separate them into three vertical columns, making spaces where the arrows indicate in the diagram. Look at the elements, the Major Arcana and court cards, inversions and repeated numbers in each column.

The right hand column (one/two, seven/eight and thirteen/fourteen) indicates the background or backbone of the querent's life. The middle column (three/four, nine/ten, fifteen/sixteen) is the mainstream of the querent's life, and receives the primary focus of her attention. The main tasks of her life are represented here, though doing the necessary preparation as indicated by the previous column is also important. The left hand column (five/six, eleven/twelve, seventeen/eighteen) represents the direction the querent is heading, the fate she is creating for herself. Any weakness in her character may be apparent here, especially in cards five and six, and her spiritual potential, her highest ideal or current

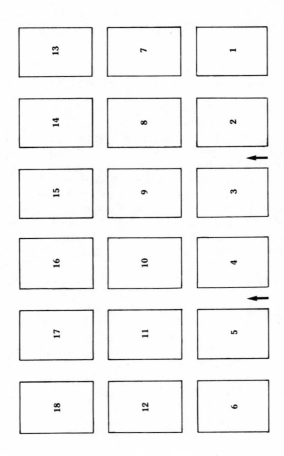

The Eighteen Card Gypsy Method

goal is likely to be reflected in cards seventeen and eighteen.
To move from one state to the other she must do the work
indicated in cards eleven and twelve, and in the spread
generally.

Imagine a lemniscate laid over the cards, one edge at card
one, the other at card eighteen, the centre of power lying
between cards nine and ten. To read this spread adequately
you must let your intuition flow, allowing the patterns of energy
to present their interlinking matrices to your consciousness.
The refinement of your perception and your powers of
interpretation are exercised and developed in reading this
spread.

THE LUNAR CROSS

This spread shows the querent's karma and is also called the
Mystic Cross. Loosely speaking, karma is the fate we create for
ourselves, the range of possibilities we make available to
ourselves in our lives through our actions. Actions in this sense
include what we do and also what we feel, think and believe.
Karma or fate is never fixed but influenced by us at each
moment of our existence. We do have free will within the
limitations of our potential in each lifetime. This spread can
help the querent to see the most helpful course to take to
exercise her free will and move her life along her chosen
course. This spread is read without significators.

The influences from the unseen world and the querent's
already created karma join with her actions in the world today
to create the karma of her future. The querent's essential
karmic nature, the aspect of her character central to the
working out of her current karmic experience is the pivot of this
symbolic spread. Spend sufficient time with this pattern to feel
any energies that may be set in motion.

Lay out the cards as in the diagram. Turn up cards one to
three to see the influences of the unseen world that are assisting
the querent in working out her karma. Card one is furthest
away from the querent and hence its effects may be more
muted than cards two and three, whose influences are
progressively more direct. Next turn up cards eight, nine and
ten. These cards show the past karma created by the querent,
which is acting on her now and shaping her choices, Again, card
eight is more distant than cards nine or ten. Now turn up card
four which shows how the querent has put these forces
together to create herself in her current karmic reality. Take
some time reading this card, and refer back to it when all the

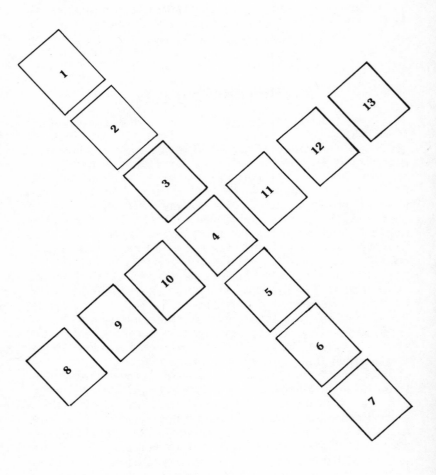

The Lunar Cross

cards have been revealed and interpreted.

Next turn up cards five, six and seven. These cards indicate the ways in which the querent is currently responding to the karmic pressures in her life. Cards eleven, twelve and thirteen indicate the fate the querent is creating for herself. Remember, if the querent doesn't like the look of the future she can alter it by making changes in the present. This is the challenge of free will.

THE STONE CIRCLE

This spread is used to look at the present phase of the querent's life. The cards are cooked, shuffled, cut once and laid in the pattern shown in the diagram. Begin by reading the significators. S_1 is chosen by the querent from the fanned deck *after* the spread has been laid on the cloth. This card represents the querent. S_2 is the card cut to by the querent after you finished shuffling, before the spread was laid. This card represents the cosmic forces acting on the querent, the unseen energies surrounding her. Next turn up cards one to four. Number one is the roots of the present phase. If this is the querent's first-ever Tarot reading this card also shows the querent's karmic memory. Card two is the recent past. Looking at the stone circle as a wheel, this card shows the energy which brought the querent into the present phase. Card three represents her conscious preoccupations. If this card appears to be unconnected to the rest of the spread it indicates a mental obsession, a worry which is distracting the querent from what is really going on in her life. This nagging concern is likely to be draining her energy and you can reassure the querent by reminding her of the superficiality of mind trips. If the querent's energies are integrated this card will relate to the midheaven in her natal astrological chart. The fourth card, remembering the wheel, represents the energies that will take the querent out of the present phase and into the next one. In this sense it represents the near future, but should be viewed as a card of movement, not a static culmination.

Next turn up cards five, six and seven. These represent the inner resources available to the querent in her present phase. These energies have been with the querent throughout her life and are particularly active at the present time. These cards generally correspond to her natal sun, moon and rising sign, and the querent is likely to be consciously aware of these energies. If all three cards are of the same element, the querent must focus on that energy in the present phase, to compensate for a previous deficiency, or unblock some channels in order to

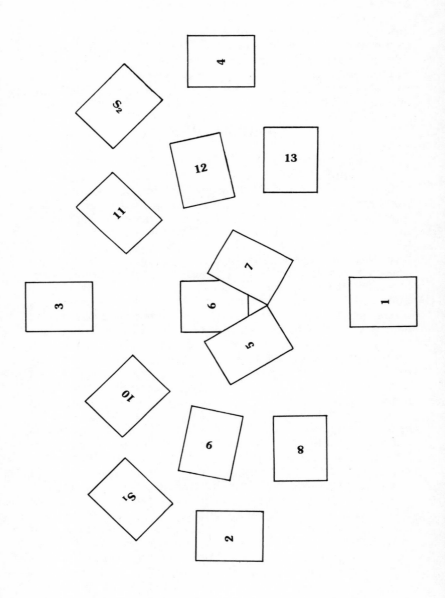

The Stone Circle

be more effective and to express herself more fully in life. She will need the energy of that element to deal with the challenges at hand. Pause here and ask the querent if she has any questions before you proceed.

Now turn up cards eight to thirteen. These represent the present phase, the first three being the querent's relationship with herself (eight, nine, ten), and the second three (eleven, twelve, thirteen) being her relationship with the outside world. The first three generally follow one another in time, eight being what is going on with the querent at the time of the reading. Cards eleven, twelve and thirteen also progress sequentially in time, and occur simultaneously with cards eight, nine and ten. Thus card eleven shows what is going on with the querent in her relationship with the outside world at the time of the reading, card twelve is coming up soon in that arena at the same time that her inner life moves into the experiences indicated by card nine. The end of the present phase is indicated by card ten which shows the achievements in personal growth and card thirteen which shows the outcome of the querent's present dealings with the world.

Card thirteen together with card four shows how the querent will move into the future. When interpreting the spread, read the six round the circle sequentially to establish the rhythm of the movement before pairing them to examine reflections of the inner in the outer. Also look to see if cards ten and eleven form a strong relationship to card three which may outweigh the significance of the pairing. In this case, the cards will indicate that the querent is joining the direction of her personal development with her conscious preoccupations and the way she expresses herself in the outside world, to generate a unity of intention with an intensity which will bring success to her efforts.

If the querent is going through a particularly intense time the present phase may last only a fortnight or, more generally, one moon cycle. Otherwise a phase is usually about three months, and can be seen as seasonal. The querent herself may already be aware of the length of the cycles in her life and not need to ask about duration. And, of course, phases also last a number of years, during which time the general pattern will recur in various readings.

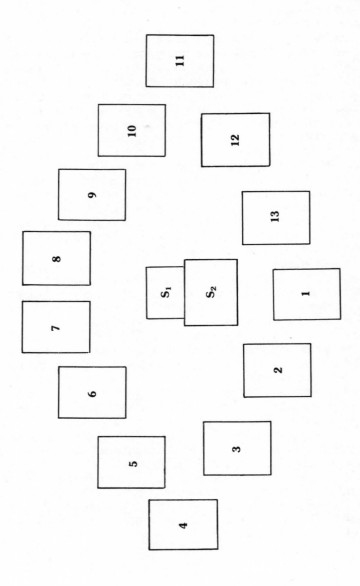

The Zodiac Spread

THE ZODIAC SPREAD

This spread is used to see the year ahead. Shuffle the deck and have the querent cut once. Place thirteen cards face down in an oval on the cloth. Then fan the deck and have the querent select one card. This is S_1, the card representing the querent for the year, and should be read first. After reading this card have the querent place it face up in the centre of the spread. Take the card the querent cut to and place it face up across the first significator. This card is S_2 and represents the cosmic energies which will surround the querent for the year. After you have read the significators, turn up cards one to four. These represent the next three to three-and-a-half months, though it is more helpful to think in terms of seasons or transits of the signs of the zodiac.

Next read cards five to eight, then nine to eleven and lastly twelve and thirteen. It is also possible to read cards one to three, then four to seven, next eight to ten, and then eleven to thirteen. This is entirely a matter of choice for the reader and should depend on your feel of the energies in a spread. If the third card is a five, or another card of difficulty, I tend to turn up number four to see what resolution may be offered before I begin to read the year. Remember that it is essential to leave the querent with a feeling of optimism about her coming year.

THE THIRTEEN CARD PYRAMID

This spread is used to look at future trends and reveals the energy patterns likely to emerge over the next six to twenty-four months in the querent's life. Cook, shuffle and cut the deck in the usual way, and lay out thirteen cards in a pyramid as shown in the diagram. Next, present the fanned deck to the querent to select an individual significator, and read this card for her. Now take the card cut from the bottom of the deck and read it as the cosmic significator, representing the unseen forces around the querent.

After you have read the significators, turn up cards one, five, nine and thirteen to see the general direction of the spread. Comment on these cards only if you feel it is necessary. The more you say the less the querent will remember. Words carry power; do not use them wastefully. Now turn up all the cards in the spread and read them in turn. When you have finished ask the querent if she has any questions.

When you are satisfied that she is ready to proceed, separate cards five, six and seven into a small pyramid on your left-hand side and cards one, two and ten into a similar one on

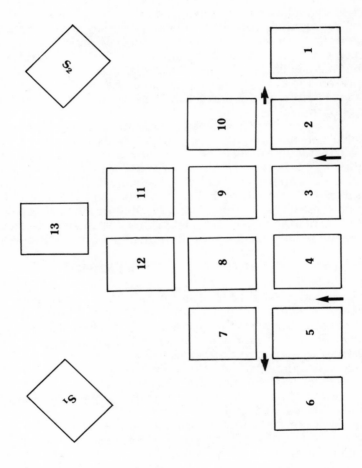

The Thirteen Card Pyramid

the opposite side. The left-hand pyramid indicates what will be going on in the querent's inner life during the period being looked at. The right-hand pyramid shows what the querent will be seen to be doing in her life. The central column shows the core energies the querent will be dealing with, card thirteen indicating where the current trend of her behaviour will take her if she carries on in her present manner.

As usual, look at repeating numbers, inversions, court cards and Major Arcana cards, and be sure to count the elements. Your task is to help guide the querent to a successful integration of her energies so that she may realise her full potential in life.

THE TWENTY-ONE CARD PYRAMID

The Twenty-One Card Pyramid is used to look at future trends over the next two to five years in the querent's life. Significators may be read with this spread if you wish. When you have cooked and shuffled the deck, had the querent cut, laid the spread and optionally read the significators, turn up cards one, five, nine, thirteen, seventeen and twenty-one to see the general trend of developments. When you have had a look at these indicators and feel ready to proceed, turn up cards one to eight.

It is possible that the first four or five cards will indicate the querent's past, the present appearing only at the end of the first line rather than at the beginning of it. This is more likely if the spread is the first one used in a consultation, and in this case the length of time covered by the spread is necessarily reduced. In order to have the future indicated by card one of this spread it is best to precede this reading with the Stone Circle spread, looking at the recent past and directly at the present and near future, before attempting to divine the patterns further ahead in the querent's life. However, if the cards insist on looking backward to begin with this is obviously an important part of the querent's future development and must be accepted as such. This aspect must then be integrated into your interpretation.

Next, read cards nine to fourteen, turning them all up at once and reading them sequentially. Follow on with cards fifteen to eighteen and finish with cards nineteen to twenty-one. You may, depending on the 'feel' of card eighteen, want to turn up cards fifteen to twenty-one together, to see the end pattern before you begin reading the third line.

When you have read all the cards in turn, ask the querent if

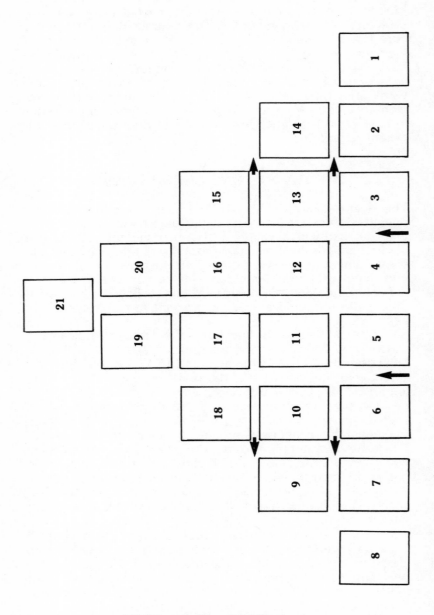

The Twenty-One Card Pyramid

she has any questions. After you have dealt with these, separate the spread where indicated by arrows in the diagram, creating a smaller pyramid at each side of a central pillar. The pyramid on your left-hand side indicates the developments in the querent's inner life during the period of time revealed by the spread. The pyramid at your right hand indicates what will be seen to be going on in the querent's life in the outside world. Consider the bottom line in each group to indicate the base on which the querent will be building in developing the facilities indicated in the pyramid. If the first few cards showed the past, this information will be particularly relevant in discerning the meaning of the 'outer' pyramid, and the 'inner' pyramid will then be likely to be based on work the querent is doing at the time of the reading. Also consider the court cards, Major Arcana cards, inversions and repeated numbers as well as the balance of elements in interpreting the progress the querent will make in her inner and outer lives, as revealed by these side pyramids, in her future. Then look at the central core of the querent's life for the next few years. Again, consider the usual guidelines for interpretation.

Remember in examining future trends that, if the querent is not happy with what she sees, she can change her future by altering her responses to the situations in her life, beginning from today.

THE SOLAR CROSS

This spread is also known as the Celtic Cross and is best used to answer a question. The querent may need help in formulating the question, or she may be clear on the matter in her own mind and prefer not to share the question with the reader. When the querent has formulated the question about her own life as specifically as possible, have her choose a number. Then, while she is concentrating on the question, shuffle to her number. When she has cut the cards, deal the twelve cards of this spread directly off from the top of the deck.

Card one indicates present forces acting in regard to the question. Card two shows forces crossing the question, possibly energies antagonistic to it. Card three represents what is weighing on the matter; card four is underlying it, possibly the root of the matter or the hidden truth about the querent in relation to the question. Card five shows what is behind the matter and the recent past. Card six shows what is immediately ahead for the querent in regard to the question. Pause here to see if the querent has any questions.

Now turn up card seven. This shows the querent in

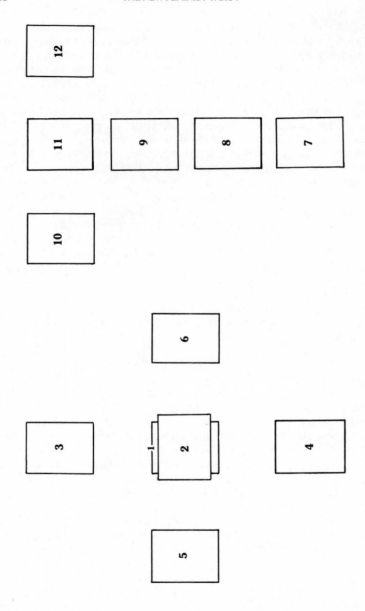

The Solar Cross

relation to the question. Card eight shows the environment in which the question is being asked. Card nine shows the querent's hopes and fears in regard to the question. Cards ten, eleven and twelve indicate the outcome. If these cards, especially card twelve, are moving cards such as the Wheel of Fortune or the six of cups, the matter is not yet decided and the outcome cannot be foreseen at the time of the reading.

THE SEVEN CARD KEY

The Seven Card key is used to answer a simple question that may remain at the end of a reading, or as a means of summarizing a full consultation. It is also the best spread to use when one is in a phase of consulting the Tarot compulsively, unable to think clearly about even small matters in one's life. This spread can be read with or without significators. If you use significators, S_1 represents the querent in relation to the question, especially its outcome, and S_2 is the cosmic energy around the question. After you have shuffled the querent cuts four times to the left. S_1 is the card on top of the penultimate (one before the last) pile. S_2 is the card left on top of the deck *before* it was cut. In order to identify these significators it is important to watch the querent cut the deck. As you restack the deck, turn the significators up in front of the querent and read them. Then lay the seven cards.

Turn up cards five and three and read them as this helps the querent in answering the question. Cards six and two indicate the unexpected in relation to the question. Cards seven and one are the outcome. Card four shows the querent's relation to the question at the present time, the time of the reading. When all the cards have been read, look at cards five through seven together, to see the querent's inner life in relation to the question. Cards three, two and one show the querent's outer life, or personality in the world, in relation to the question.

Because of the brevity of this spread, it is one of the few where reversals may be meaningfully interpreted as representing negative energies, or saying 'no'.

THE HORSESHOE SPREAD

This twenty-one card spread gives an overall picture of the querent, her situation and temperament, and what lies ahead for her. After shuffling, have the querent cut the deck. If the deck is cut once you may want to read the card cut to as the significator, representing the cosmic energy surrounding the

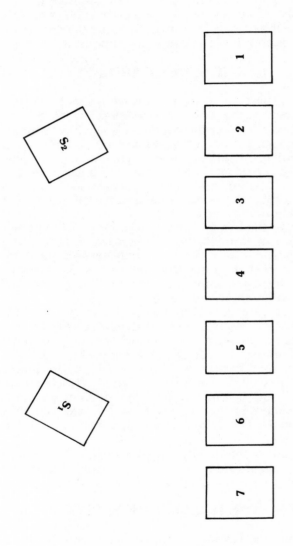

The Seven Card Key

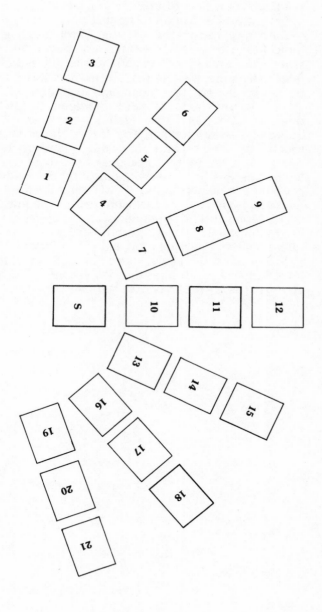

The Horseshoe Spread

reading. Then deal out seven groups of three cards each as indicated in the diagram. The first three indicate the self, the second three the querent's home. Cards seven, eight and nine indicate her desires while cards ten, eleven and twelve show what she expects to happen. Cards thirteen, fourteen and fifteen show the unexpected. The immediate future is indicated by cards sixteen, seventeen and eighteen while long-term influences are shown by cards nineteen, twenty and twenty-one. As with the Gypsy Method, the first row shows the querent's baser energies, the forces she is most directly in touch with. The second arc of the horseshoe indicates those energies the querent is conscious of and deals with on a mental level. It is this level of her being that she believes is being presented to the world, though of course the first layer contains her actual points of contact with reality. The third card in each group represents her finer ideals, and energies she must stretch to touch though they are part of her realizable potential. The querent should be reminded that cards thirteen to twenty-one indicate what is likely given her present situation and intentions. She can alter the developments in her life if she changes her own behaviour. We create our own fate.

AFTERWORD : THE DIANIC CRAFT

From Paleolithic or Old Stone Age times, people have revered nature and lived in harmony with the elements. They recognized the creative power of wymn in the cosmos, from the watery abyss of the primal void or universal mother, through the fruitfulness of youthful maidens and aging crones, to the all-consuming fiery hag, animated throughout by life-giving spirit. The beliefs and practices of this way of life are called the Craft. Wicca is the name given to those who practise and teach the Craft. From this derives the word witch.

Witch is still a very emotive word today and, even among feminists, it can arouse fear. Though we talk loosely and in political terms of reclaiming our power, few among us have the courage or inclination to discipline necessary to develop our potential. Many of us have been persecuted, even tortured and murdered, in previous lives for following the Craft and so are hesitant to do so openly today. The scorn of our sisters also inhibits us. But, for a few, the pull of our inheritance is too strong to deny.

Within the tradition of Wicca there are many different paths. Dianic Wicca, dedicated to Diana, Horned Huntress of the Night, Protectress of Womyn, is a path of autonomous womyn-loving womyn. Feminist Wicca, witchcraft with a feminist politic, has been growing and expanding in recent years, and a number of covens have been initiated in America by Z. Budapest, an hereditary Hungarian witch. I was initiated into her Susan B. Anthony Coven Number One on a winter solstice during a visit to America in 1973. As the Manifesto of the Coven says: 'We believe that without a secure grounding in womon's spiritual strength there will be no victory for us. We are committed to teaching wimmin how to organize themselves as witches and to sharing our traditions with wimmin. We are opposed to teaching our magic and our craft to men.' Groves, groups of womyn practising the Dianic Craft, are growing again in Britain. For now we, the womyn, are the trees, increasing our strength and giving witness to our determination to survive, to be free and to serve goddess. Some day we will again have land on which to live in open expression of our beliefs, celebrating skyclad amidst Diana's sacred groves. By returning goddess to the world through our recognition of Her continuing existence we are creating the necessary conditions for our liberation.

8. Major Arcana Card XXI — The World

Much of our tradition has been obscured over the centuries. The oppression we have suffered made it difficult to pass on our teachings to younger generations. The persecutions of witches forced many of us into hiding, and caused us to mask our tools in symbols which could only be read by the initiated. Study, meditation and the regular celebration of rituals lead to the development of the insight and powers of discernment that enable us to reclaim the ancient wisdom of wymn. Tarot is one of the tools we use for this work.

GLOSSARY

ACHIEVE — to perform, accomplish; to reach by exercise, do successfully.

ALCHEMY — science of transmuting elements, especially lead to gold; method of seeking the elixir of perpetual youth; process of mysterious change.

ARCANA — chests; shut in, hidden; secrets, mysteries.

ASTRAL — of, from, like the stars; belonging to the stars; the astral body is one of the four nonmaterial humun forms which together comprise our aura.

AURA — the energy emanating from and enveloping a living body.

AVATAR — teacher; spiritual guide.

AWARENESS — knowing through the senses; consciousness of; informed.

BELIEF — an opinion or doctrine accepted as true.

CELTIC — of the Celts, a people of Wales, Scotland, Ireland, the West of England and Brittany reputedly magical.

CEREMONY — outward form.

COMMUNION — a sharing; an intimate spiritual relationship.

COMPASSION — deep sympathy; a fiery sensation of detached love, usually a warmer feeling than pity.

COMPETENCE — ability, skill, fitness.

COMPREHEND — to make sense of with the mind; to take in; to understand, to grasp mentally, decipher; to fathom.

CONSECRATE — to set apart; to devote or dedicate especially to religious use.

COSMIC — characteristic of the universe and its changes. Cosmic harmony is the music of the spheres.

COSMOS — the universe as an harmonious whole.

DECK — a pack of cards or part of a pack.

DEVA — a spirit; an air elemental.

DEVOTION — a combination of affection and commitment, possibly implying subservience.

DISCERN — to make out clearly; to perceive or recognize, especially differences.

DIVINATION — foretelling the future by intuitive perception.

ELEMENT — any of the four substances that constitute physical matter according to the ancients.

ELEMENTAL — a creature of an element : siren or undine, sylph or deva, gnome or dwarf, elf or fairy.

ELF — a magic sprite of woods and hills; a fire elemental.

EMBLEM — a visible symbol; an object or picture representing an idea or an object different from itself; a picture with a moral allegory.

EMPATHY — ability to enter into another's emotional state.

ENCHANT — to cast a spell over, bewitch; to charm.

ENERGY — inherent power; capacity of a material body or of radiation to do work.

ESOTERIC — intended for or understood by only a few, or by a minority.

ESTEEM — to value; to have a favourable opinion of.

ETERNAL — existing through all time; without beginning or end; everlasting; perpetual.

ETHERIC — of the nonmaterial medium surrounding and enclosing physical bodies; the etheric body is one of the four comprising the aura.

EVOLUTION — gradual working out, development, unfolding or unrolling.

FAIRY — graceful sprite of the countryside; a fire elemental.

FAITH — unquestioning belief; trust, confidence or reliance as in 'Do you have faith in womyn?'

FANTASY — a series of mental images moved along by one's will.

FORCE — influence producing result; impetus; exertion of power; strength, energy, vigour.

GEOMANCY — earth divination, insight through interpretation of signs in and from the earth.

GNOME — small creature dwelling in the earth and guarding its treasures; dwarf; earth elemental.

GNOSIS — positive knowing in spiritual matters.

GREAT — a concept created by patriarchy which will disappear with it, meaning much more than ordinary, chief, weighty. Using this concept conditions the mind to hierarchy.

GROWTH — development, evolution.

GUIDE — to point out the way for; direct on a course; conduct.

HARMONY — a combination of moving parts into a proportionate or rhythmical whole; a fitting well together, connectedness; peaceable and agreeable relations, concord. (*See also* Cosmic harmony.)

HEATHEN — usually a term of abuse signifying an irreligious person, said insultingly of pagans.

HUMILITY — absence of pride.

IDEAL — a conception of something in its most perfect or desirable form; best idea.

IMAGE — a representation or visual impression; a likeness or a mental picture; an idea or representation which forms a still picture of itself.

IMAGINATION — the ability to form symbols and images in the mind, the creative ability; the ability to understand and appreciate phenomena and concepts which have not been previously experienced.

INCANTATION — a formula of words said or sung for purposes of enchantment; magical chanting.

INDICATE — to suggest, point to, direct attention to; to signify, betoken, intimate.

INITIATE — one who, in a secret ceremony, has been introduced to knowledge or admitted to a mystery or secret society.

INTEGRATION — act or process of weaving into a whole.

INTELLECTUAL — using the thinking principle and rational powers of the mind to perceive and understand.

INTENSE — concentrated, very strong, vivid.

INTERPRET — to explain the meaning of, make understandable; to show the significance of.

INTUITION — the power of the mind for immediate perception; immediate knowing or learning without the use of reasoning or analysis; instantaneous apprehension using the powers of the psyche.

INVERTED — turned upside down, reversed, turned inwards.

INVOCATION — the act or form of addressing in prayer, calling upon earnestly or solemnly; to request assistance of, summon by charm or incantation.

KARMA — the totality of a person's actions determining the course of her existence; the interaction of past present and future in the choices made by each individual throughout their existence.

KNOWLEDGE — familiarity gained by experience; assured belief; awareness, understanding. Also sagacity, skill, ability.

LEMNISCATE — figure of eight on its side, a symbol meaning infinity.

LOGIC — structure for thinking; a rigid form for the progression of reasoning developed by solar patriarchy and based on cause and effect; the masculist science which deals with the criteria of valid thought.

LUMINARY — a source of light, especially a heavenly body.

LUNAR — pertaining to the moon, belonging to or referring to the moon.

MAGIC — producing effects and/or controlling events by ritual; a sense of powerful mystery.

MASCULIST — one who believes in, advocates or lives according to the values of male supremacy.

MATRIARCH — a womon who is head and ruler of her family and desdendents; a woman who governs.

MEAN — to intend to express, denote, convey, signify, indicate.

MUNDANE — ordinary; of the everyday world; not sacred, unconsecrated.

MYSTERY — something secret or obscure.

MYSTIC — a person or thing having spiritual symbolism or significance; an experience of spiritual truth through intuition, usually while in meditation.

NUMEROLOGY — study of the value of numbers, especially their esoteric or occult meaning; divination by numbers.

OCCULT — hidden, concealed, esoteric. Occult sciences are alchemy, astrology, numerology, magic etc.

PACK — a number of similar or related things or beings, usually in a group or bundle; a complete set of cards.

PAGAN — someone whose spiritual or religious belief is poly- or pan-theistic, especially one who personifies and honours the forces of nature and celebrates the Sabbats; an individual with reverence for the earth, her creatures and the natural cycle of life and the seasons.

PARANYM — word that has been corrupted into an opposite and untruthful meaning, e.g. 'witch'.

PARTICULAR — specific, singular, unique, special.

PERCEPTION — consciousness, awareness; intuitive insight.

PITY — sorrow felt for another's suffering or misfortune, usually slightly contemptuous.

POLARITY — contrary tendencies, qualities, powers, etc; opposedness of aspect or tendency.

POTENTIAL — latent, existing in possibility; powers or resources not yet developed.

POWER — ability to do anything; capacity for producing an effect.

PRAYER — an earnest request, supplication.

PRIDE — excessive self-esteem usually accompanied by an inability to accept criticism; haughtiness, arrogance, conceit.

PROFANE — irreverant, contemptuous of the sacred.

PROPHET — a person who speaks as though under divine guidance; inspired teacher poet or preacher; one who foretells events.

PROPORTIONATE — arranged in an harmonious relationship,

PSYCHE — that part of the knowing Self which synergizes mind emotions and physical experience. Sometimes confused with the soul or desire body. (See also Intuition.)

PSYCHIC — able to perceive directly in and through the psyche; sensitive to forces beyond the physical world.

QABALA — the Hebrew mystical tradition; an occult religious philosophy based on this science. (Also spelt KABALA and CABALA.)

QUERENT — someone who queries or asks.

QUINTESSENTIAL — pure concentrated essence especially of anything immaterial.

RANDOM — haphazard; without plan, aim or method.

READER — one who observes or studies and interprets.

READING — an interpretation.

REALISATION — making real; bringing into being; to achieve, obtain; active knowing.

REASON — to analyse; the ability to think and to form judgements dispassionately.

RELIGION — a set of beliefs and practices or system of thought about the truth of the cosmos. Organized religions require fixed forms of observance. All patriarchal religions posit hierarchical cosmic structures.

RELIGIOUS — someone who expresses their beliefs about reality in a consistent way of life through their philosophy, conduct and/or ritual observance. Any philosophy, conduct or observance which derives from such beliefs.

REPRESENT — to serve as a symbol for; to present or picture to the mind.

RESONANCE — resounding; sonority; sympathetic vibration; re-echoing.

RESPECT — to honour; to feel esteem for; regard.

REVEAL — to make known by divine agency or inspiration; to disclose or make visible as if drawing back a veil.

REVERENCE — to regard or treat with respect; to venerate.

REVERSAL — being turned the other way about as upside down; inversion.

RITUAL — a formal or informal ceremony repeated at cyclic intervals.

SACRED — dedicated, especially in a religious sense; regarded with respect and reverence; venerated.

SECRET — concealed; a thing guarded against discovery or observation; secluded.

SEQUENTIAL — following; successive; moving in regular

order.

SHOW — to make visible, to cause or allow to appear to be seen or known; display.

SIGNIFICATOR — a person or thing that suggests or expresses special or hidden meaning.

SIGNIFY — to be a sign or indication.

SIREN — a female sea creature who draws other beings to her with the magic of her music; a water elemental.

SOLAR — pertaining to the sun.

SOUL — the emotional or moral nature of a humun being said to be seated in the heart; the astral or desire body.

SPIRITUAL — of, concerned with, devoted to or imbued with faith in an inexplicable meaning of existence; pertaining to the vital principle.

SPIRITUALITY — the state or part of one's being concerned with eternal existence, often of religious nature.

SPREAD — a display, a layout or exhibit.

SPRITE — a fire elemental.

STRIVE — to make efforts; to endeavour earnestly; to struggle.

SUIT — a series, a sequence; a set of cards of one kind.

SYLPH — a spirit, an air elemental.

SYMBOL — a thing accepted as representing another because it in some way suggests the essential and often spiritual quality of the other; an image used to represent something abstract.

SYMBOLIC — serving as a symbol; expressed in symbol(s).

SYMBOLIZE — to typify, stand for, represent.

SYMPATHY — affinity; agreement in quality; ability to relate to another's emotional state; goodwill based on agreement or understanding.

SYNCHRONICITY — the quality of being or happening at the same time, of having the same period or phase; simultaneity; occurring together.

TEACHER — one who imparts knowledge, instructs, explains or trains.

THINK — to exercise the mind; to reason or reflect; to use mental faculties to form ideas, images, etc.

TOOL — an instrument for achieving any purpose, e.g. an emblem.

TRADITION — a convention established by habitual practice; a long-established custom or practice.

TREND — general direction or tendency; a drift or disposition.

UNDERSTAND — to know thoroughly; to grasp without explanation.

UNDINE — female water elemental.

UNIVERSAL — of the whole of existence, of the totality of

creation.

VARIOUS — several, many, different.

VENERATE — to honour; to show deep respect.

VISUALIZATION — an image or continuous sequence of events appearing to one's inner eye and moved by the psyche, imagination or inner guide.

WILL — strong purpose or intention; power of choosing or determining.

WITNESS — give proof or evidence.

WORSHIP — fervent esteem; adoration; submissive respect; an attitude and/or emotion encouraged in women by patriarchy.

This glossary was compiled from *Chamber's Everyday Dictionary*, *Webster's New World Dictionary of the American Language*, and from my own head.

BIBLIOGRAPHY

Below is a list of the books on Tarot I have delved into over the years. I have also been influenced in my interpretations by a number of other books that explore various theories about the meaning of life, and the interface between spirituality and politics. Many of these are listed in the Bibliography of *Further Thoughts on Feminism or What Is To Be Done*, my previous book completed in 1979. Basically though my understanding of Tarot comes from my meditations on the cards and my intuitive interpretations when reading spreads for myself and others.

BUDAPEST, Z.   *The Feminist Book of Lights and Shadows*, (Luna Publications).

BUTLER, Bill.   *The Definitive Tarot*, (Rider).

CASE, Paul Foster.   *Tarot: Key to the Wisdom of the Ages.*

CROWLEY, Aleister.   *Tarot Divination.*

— *The Book of Thoth*, (Weiser).

DOUGLAS, Alfred.   *The Tarot*, (Penguin Books).

GARDNER, Richard.   *The Tarot Speaks.*

— *Evolution Through The Tarot.*

GEARHART, Sally and RENNIE, Susan. *A Feminist Tarot*, (Persephone Press).

GRAY, Eden.   *A Complete Guide To The Tarot*, (Bantam Books).

HUSON, Paul.   *The Devil's Picture Book.*

KAPLAN, Stuart.   *Encyclopedia of Tarot.*

LIND, Frank.   *How To Understand The Tarot*, (Aquarian Press).

OUSPENSKY, P.D.   *The Symbolism of The Tarot*, (Dover Publications).

PAPUS (Dr. Gerard Encausse)   *The Tarot of the Bohemians.*

POLLACK, Rachel.   *78 Degrees of Wisdom*, (Aquarian Press).

POTTS, Billie.   *A New Women's Tarot*, (Elf & Dragon Press).
SADHU, Mouni.   *The Tarot.*
STUART, Micheline.   *The Tarot: Path to Self-Development*,
   (Shambhala Publications).
WAITE, A.E.   *The Pictorial Key to The Tarot*, (Rider).

MAJOR CORRESPONDENCES

I	The Alchemist (Magician)	Aries	Magician (I)
II	The Initiate (Priestess)	Pisces	High Priestess (II)
III	Love	Gemini	Lovers (VI)
IV	The Elder	Capricorn	Emperor (IV)
V	The Chariot (Self-Discipline)	Sagittarius	Chariot (V or VII)
VI	The Matriarch	Taurus	Empress (III)
VII	Keeper of the Mysteries (The Prophet)	Uranus	Hierophant (VII or V)
VIII	Strength (Courage)	Venus	Strength (VIII or XI)
IX	Justice (The Truth)	Libra	Justice (IX or XI or VIII)
X	Wheel of Fortune	Mars	Wheel (X)
XI	The Wise Woman (Geomancer)	Virgo	Hermit (IX or XI)
XII	Hanging (Healing)	Mercury	Hanged Man (XII)
XIII	Death (Change)	Pluto	Death (XIII)
XIV	The Thunderbolt/ The Lightning Flash	Neptune	Lightning Struck Tower (XVI)
XV	Temperance	Jupiter	Temperance (XIV)
XVI	The Earth Dragon	Saturn	Devil (XV)
XVII	The Star	Aquarius	Star (XVII)
XVIII	The Moon	Cancer	Moon (XVIII)
XIX	The Sun	Leo	Sun (XIX)
XX	Judgement (Spiritual Reawakening)	Scorpio	Judgement (XX)
XXI	The World		The World (XXI)
0	The Fool		The Fool (0)

INDEX

Achaiva, 92
air, 40
Air Dragon, 80
air, key words of, 42
Alchemist, The, 32, 75, 92
alchemy, 32
Aleister Crowley Tarot, 41
Amaterasu, 89
Amazon, 40
ankh, 73
Aquarian Tarot, 18
Arinna, 89
Artemis Caryatis, 84
astrology, 32
Atlantis, 16

Bach Flower Remedies, 55
Besant, Annie, 15
Bembo, Bonafacio, 15
Blavatsky, Helena Petrovna, 15, 80
Bodhisattva of Compassion, 83
Boiardo, Count Maria, 15
BonaDea, 87
Book of Thoth, 15
B.O.T.A. (Builders of the Adytum) Tarot, 19
Budapest, Z., 17, 113
Builders of the Adytum (B.O.T.A.) Tarot, 19
Burns Parke, Jessie, 19
Butler, Bill, 18

Caduceus, 74
Cardea, 77
Cerridwen, 86
Chariot, The, 32, 78-9
Charles VI of France, 15
Christian, Paul, 16
Coleman Smith, Pamela, 17, 18
Companion, 40
Conqueror, The, 79
Constant, Abbé Alphonse Louis, 16
court cards, 40
Crowley, Aleister, 14, 15, 16, 87
Crowley, Aleister, Tarot, 19
Cups, Suit of, (Water), 44-50
cutting, 27
Cybele, Queen of Summer, 80-81

Dakini Tarot, 19
Death, 31, 84
Demeter, 74, 92
Diana, 83, 113, 114
Dianic Craft, 22, 86, 114
Douglas, Alfred, 15

earth, 41
Earth Dragon, 31, 38, 86
earth, key words of, 43
Egyptian Gypsies Tarot, 18, 78
Egyptial Tarot, 17
Eighteen Card Gypsy Method, 25, 27, 28, 95-7
Elder, The, 32, 78
elements, 40
Encausse, Dr Gerard, 14, 16
Epona, 74

Farr, Florence, 14
Fatima, 88
Feminist Tarot, A, 16
fire, 41
Fire Dragon, 85
Fire, Keeper of the, 76
fire, key words of, 44
Firth, Violet, 15
Flora, 77
Fool, The, 38, 92
Fortitude, 80
Fortune, Dion, 15, 16, 74
Foster Case, Paul, 14, 16, 19

Gaea, 87, 88
Gardner, Richard, 18, 29
Gatekeeper, The, 76
Gearhart, Sally, 16, 52
Gebelin, Antoine Court de, 16
Golden Dawn, Order of the, 14
Gonne, Maud, 14
Grainne, 87, 89
Grand Eteilla Tarot (*see also* Egyptian Gypsies Tarot), 18
Green Tara, 83
Greine, 89
Gringonneur, Jacquemin, 15
Gurdjieff, G.I., 16
gypsies, 16

Hanging, 32, 84
Harris, Frieda, 19
Hathor, Queen of Heaven, 87, 88
Hera, 37
Hippocrates, 74
Horseshoe Spread, 25, 95, 109, 111

I Ching, 89
I.J.J. Swiss Tarot, 17
Initiate, The, 32, 76